Insights Into Our Design and Purpose

Keith Carroll

Newburg, Pennsylvania

Created to Relate
by Keith Carroll
Copyright ©2016 Keith Carroll

All rights reserved. This book is protected under the copyright laws of the United States of America. This book may not be copied or reprinted for commercial gain or profit.

Unless otherwise identified, Scripture is taken from the *New American Standard Bible*, Copyright ©1960, 1962, 1963, 1968, 1971, 1973, 1975, 1977 by The Lockman Foundation.

ISBN 978-0-9860923-3-6 (print)
For Worldwide Distribution
Printed in the U.S.A.

Relate To God Press
PO Box 341
Newburg, PA 17240

Special Thanks

*For the inspiring contributions of
my wife, Nancy; Thelma and Gary Diehl;
Delores Ocker; and Alice and Rocky Rockwell*

*For the invaluable editorial skills
of Brian and Kathy Banashak*

*And to Sam and Daphne Eaton,
and Glen Reed for their deeply
rewarding fellowship*

Table of Contents

Introduction *v*
1. Two Realms Sustain Us *1*
2. Body and Spirit Link Us *19*
3. Conscious Soul Informs Us *37*
4. Expressive Heart Reveals Us *55*
5. Relational Concept Connects Us *77*
6. Father's Fellowship Nurtures Us *98*
7. Will of God Directs Us *117*
8. Purpose of Life Destines Us *138*

Appendices: Keys to Understanding
I. Cold, Dark, and Evil *153*
II. Body and Flesh *158*
III. Get Understanding *163*
IV. Attitude Rules *168*
V. Mature Not Perfect *174*
VI. Called and Chosen *178*
VII. Light of Life *182*
VIII. What Is Faith? *187*

About the Author *195*
Additional Resources *197*

Introduction

We really are wonderfully made! So, what does God desire to accomplish in our lives and those of everyone around us? We invite you to embark on a journey of discovery to understand God's creative intention. *Created to Relate* helps us discover the mystery behind why we exist.

God created the material universe as a place to birth and initially nurture the greatest of His creations: mankind. He created us as a composite of both the natural and spiritual realities for a very specific purpose. *Created to Relate* will provide fresh light on what is meant to be created in the "image and likeness" of God. It helps us understand the difference between our spirit and our soul, and also learn how to partake of fellowship in our heavenly Father's presence.

You will see the clear difference between what we are as a functioning being (body, soul, and spirit) and who we are as a person (character, attitude, and personality). There is so much more to the human heart than you may have previously thought.

God desires to lead us through our life experiences. He provides guidance and insight through the inspiration of Scripture, from the life of Jesus Christ, and by His abiding presence. He remolds us into the delight of His heart as we seek to personally know Him and experience the fellowship of His presence.

While no one can fully know or understand God, we can understand His heart and ways, especially when we approach Him as our loving Father. The more we understand the heart and mind of God, the more effective we become in sharing His love in all our relationships. Scripture says more than forty times that we can know, teach, and walk in the ways of God. Jesus made it clear that this is not only possible but also achievable:

Ask, and it will be given to you; seek, and you will find; knock, and it will be opened to you. For everyone who asks receives, and he who seeks finds, and to him who knocks it will be opened...If you...know how to give good gifts to your children, how much more shall your Father who is in heaven give...to those who ask Him! (Matthew 7:7-8)

Each of us can yield to God and become one with His purpose for our life. As we learn to become all that God made us to be, our life will be filled with a greater sense of value and profound satisfaction.

The ancient Greek philosopher, Socrates, is quoted as saying, "Know thyself." *Created to Relate* is based on a much more reliable source of wisdom, the Bible. Let's begin!

Chapter 1

Two Realms Sustain Us

Years ago Mac was in a meeting where he had an extraordinary experience. Please be aware that by this time he was a trained minister/teacher and God had blessed many through his ministry. The following is his story:

This was before air conditioning became the norm. Listening to the minister speak about the Fatherhood of God, I found myself a bit hot and bored, so I dozed off a few times. As the message concluded, we were instructed to close our eyes and imagine ourselves in heaven. We were to visualize walking up to the throne of God and getting up on God's lap, as a child would with their father. I thought this was a bit silly, but began to do as instructed.

I saw myself approach the throne. When I got to the throne I climbed up and sat on God's right leg. Soon I began to realize I was on the wrong side. Without knowing why, I jumped down and as I climbed upon the left side I began to realize this was not just my imagination. As I got comfortable His arm held me close and I dozed off. As I awoke I noticed the other hand was almost clenched into a fist and I dozed again. Then I heard the minister say, "OK we are done," and I returned to my conscious self.

Immediately someone jumped up and told about their experience. Then another followed suit, then another. I realized everyone was relating their experience and that I would be expected to do the same. In a panic I began recalling what had happened to me.

All of a sudden insight burst upon me. God had held me close to His heart and I was so comforted that I dozed off. The other hand was poised to deal with anyone who would dare interrupt our close time together. In that instant my heart broke as I realized God was even better than my natural father. God deeply cared for me. Since that day, I have relished the fact that God is my heavenly Father. He is even better than I could have imagined.

— *Richard B. McDaniel Sr. (Mac)*

David was king in Israel from 1018 to 968 B.C. Although he was an imperfect man, Scripture records he had a heart after God (1 Samuel 13:14). David composed most of the Psalms of the Bible. When he thought about the majesty of God, he asked the question:

> *What is man that You* [God] *take thought of him, and the son of man that You care for him?* (Psalms 8:4; 144:3)

Even David wondered about God's nature. Honest questions

are healthy because they are simply our requests for more insight. They can prepare us to more fully comprehend and develop better understanding. So we ask with David: Who is God and what has He created in man that He should have any caring thought for us?

In the Beginning—God

There was a time when nothing existed but God alone. In fact, time as we know it did not even exist. There were no galaxies, stars, or planets—not even one! There was just God! Close your eyes and let that sink in for a minute. God! Are you feeling His awesomeness?

The One who identified Himself as "I AM WHO I AM" (Exodus 3:14) apparently has always existed, and as the Eternal One, He always will. His existence transcends the realm of time and space He created. Also notice He says, "WHO I AM." God is a who—a person.

Scripture describes God as a supernatural being: eternal, omnipresent, omnipotent, omniscient, and invisible. In other words, God is a Spirit being that is all powerful, perceives all, is always present everywhere, and exists in a spirit realm that has no beginning.

God is the Eternal Spirit who created the material universe with its time and space progressions. He has always existed in the spirit dimension, a realm the natural eye cannot see.

Scripture also identifies God as our heavenly Father, the One who created us. In our beginnings, God perceived of us as offspring He would birth into existence and parent us as children into His own image and likeness.

> *Then God said, "Let Us make man in Our image, according to Our likeness"* (Genesis 1:26).

Jesus spoke often of God as his Father and encouraged us to related to God as our Father.

> *Pray, then, in this way: "Our Father who is in heaven, hallowed be Your name"* (Matthew 6:9).

Surely we can't pin down the nature of God as if He can be analyzed or calibrated. God is not an object. The more we understand light and time, the more humbled and in awe we are when we read how these biblical expressions are used to describe God.

> *God is light, and in Him there is no darkness at all* (1 John 1:5).

> *God is love, and the one who abides in love abides in God, and God abides in him* (1 John 4:16).

Our life in the limitations of time and space obscures our ability to fully understand God and the spirit realm. We must first believe that God and a spirit realm really exist before we can begin to perceive and make any sense of spiritual realities.

> *Seek the LORD while He may be found; call upon Him while He is near. Let the wicked forsake his way and the unrighteous man his thoughts* (Isaiah 55:6).

God designed humanity as offspring who would grow and develop into various expressions of His image and likeness. It appears that to facilitate His concept of fathering, God designed the natural time and space universe to be an environment where He could nurture His offspring's initial birth, progressive growth, and maturing development.

Efforts to Understand

Who are we? Where did we come from? Why are we here? These are questions mankind has asked for millennia, grasping for answers from various disciplines.

Throughout history there have always been conflicting viewpoints on the existence of God and eternity, of creation, and the purpose for mankind's existence. Here are three prominent worldviews that humans have developed over the centuries:

Pagan viewpoint: Many ancient cultures perceived a superior realm as the source of our beginnings. They envisioned godlike beings, represented by stars and constellations, with very human frailties, who created our world and controlled various aspects of life. They had a god of fertility, a god of war, a god of the seas, and a whole host of other various deities. Mortals were seen as pawns in a sometimes cruel, cosmic game.

Philosophical viewpoint: The philosophers of old were mostly concerned with human thought. Socrates was a proponent of ethics. However, he didn't think virtue could be taught and believed it must be received as a gift from the gods. Plato is famous for his Republic in which he expounded on political theory and the "just man." He saw the world as defective, yet he perceived higher values that could be appreciated and pursued, such as beauty, unity, and sameness. Aristotle is considered to be the father of logic. He emphasized man's reasoning ability. Most philosophies today are based on these ancient teachings.

Scientific viewpoint: The scientific view most prominent today began to develop 100 years ago. It theorizes everything started with a very tiny, dense amount of matter that suddenly superheated and exploded in an event referred to as the "Big Bang." At that point, so the theory goes, energy, matter and the universe suddenly expanded to fill some unexplained void, and 14 billion years later has became the universe we know today. They speculate that about 3.9 billion years ago living organisms appeared out of nowhere and evolved over time through a series of evolutionary mutations into what we see today. This theory is not held by all scientists.

Biblical viewpoint: In contrast, the biblical viewpoint stands apart from these attempts to answer who we are and why are we here. The biblical perspective, although not always understood, is articulated in Scripture, was lived in the life and expressed in the words of Jesus Christ, and is revealed by the abiding presence of God.

The biblical view of creation focuses on our relationship with our Creator-Father and encourages godly relationships with one another. The natural realm's universe, which can readily be perceived by our natural senses, provides abundant evidence that the spirit realm is real and that God does exist.

> *For since the creation of the world His invisible attributes, His eternal power and divine nature, have been clearly seen, being understood through what has been made* (Romans 1:20).

Created to Relate starts with this biblical account and connects the dots of Scripture to bring fresh insight and clarity about our beginning and our destiny. If you are wondering what God has created and is making in you—read on!

Two Realms Sustain Us

Time, Space, and Eternity

The spirit realm is where God exists. The little we know about the spirit realm indicates it is far superior to the natural realm. This natural realm was created by God as a combination of enclosed and measurable spaces that exist within the immeasurable spirit realm.

In 1895, H.G. Wells wrote the classic science fiction novel, *The Time Machine*. Time travel has been a fascination of mankind ever since. In his book, Wells envisioned a dim and degraded Earth, some 800,000 years into the future.

Today, we have Dr. Who, another time traveler, who travels about from place to place and time to time. For more than 50 years, this BBC science fiction TV series has survived by rejuvenating the Doctor. To date there have been 12 Doctors. The longevity of the show is some indication of the fascination with time travel, both in Britain and America.

Some scientists believe that time travel might actually be possible. If people could go faster than the speed of light, which is calculated as 186,000 miles per second, they might actually go back in time—that is, if they could somehow survive the speed. Einstein's famous equation, $E=mc^2$, says that matter accelerated to the speed of light equals energy. So, if it were possible to achieve light speed, the would-be time traveler would likely be turned into a type of vaporous energy or be toast!

Is it possible that the interest in time travel reveals a deep-seated desire to live beyond the limitations of this life? Perhaps it comes from an inherent desire in man to experience life unrestrained by the natural realities.

For mankind, time and space are primary reference points that are continually moving and changing. The history of mankind is the record of these time and space adjustments along with our involvement.

"Space" in this natural realm is a system of containments (defined areas). Everything in space is moving and changing in their areas of activity. An example can be observed in water. Water materially exists in three stages: fluid (liquid), gas (steam and vapor) and solid (ice). The extended universe also demonstrates various stages of development.

Time measures the ongoing movements and development of the contents of the natural realm, even in what we know as outer space. These moving moments are tracked in the seconds of minutes and in the decades of centuries. We measure time on the earth by the revolving movements of our sun and moon.

In her book, *Time Peace*, Ellen Vaughn has come up with a wonderful way to blast our too-small concepts of the natural realm's time and space out of the water. She helps us contemplate time and light, two very complex elements of the created material realm, beyond our age-old perceptions. Ellen shows us how scientific findings can enlarge our perspective of God.

Ellen starts with Albert Einstein upsetting the existing perceptions of time. She says, "His discoveries showed us that the rate of time's passage is not fixed, but is in fact relative to contextual elements like velocity (rate of speed) and gravity (force of gravitation)." Time passes on earth differently than it does in outer space.

She says in her down-to-earth style, "The amount of energy available in any given bit of matter—a Tootsie Roll, a stone, an atom—is the matters mass multiplied by the fastest velocity imaginable. That would be the speed of light or c squared." Thus the formula $E=mc^2$.

That means, if we had twins and we somehow were able to send one around the world at the speed of light and the other one stayed home, the one who went jet-setting around the planet would actually come back younger than the one who stayed home. Or to put it another way, if both of those twins were wearing watches, the one who traveled at light speed would have a clock that read earlier than the one who did not leave home.

If all this seems mind-bending and perplexing, you're not alone. But it only begins to scratch the surface of opening our comprehension of how the created, material realm compares with the eternal, spiritual realm. After all, if a flesh and blood being could move at the speed of light, time would not move.

When we compare time and space concepts with the idea of eternity, we can begin to see how the progressions of time and containments of matter are quite possibly an energetic reduction of eternity. When God created this natural universe, did He in essence slow down a portion of eternity into measurable containments and progressive time frames? We will look at this possibility in a few pages.

The Heavens Beyond

We know something of the existence of God through what has been created because creation is a reflection of God:

It is He who made the earth by His power, Who established the world by His wisdom; and by His understanding He has stretched out the heavens (Jeremiah 10:12).

The heavens are telling the glory of God; they are a marvelous display of his craftsmanship. Day and night they keep on telling about God. Without a sound or word, silent in the skies, their message reaches out to all the world (Psalm 19:1-4a TLB).

The first verse of Scripture declares that before God created the earth, He created the heavens.

God created the heavens…(Genesis 1:1).

Here the word "heavens" is plural, indicating there is more than one heaven. Other scriptures make it clear there are visible heavens we see with the natural eye when we look into the sky (some near and some far). And there are heavens that relate to the unseen spirit realm that is occupied by angelic beings:

Beware not to lift up your eyes to heaven and see the sun and the moon and the stars, all the host of heaven, and be drawn away and worship them and serve them, those which the Lord your God has allotted to all the peoples under the whole heaven (Deuteronomy 4:19).

And there was war in heaven, Michael and his angels waging war with the dragon. The dragon and his angels waged war, and they were not strong enough, and there was no longer a place found for them in heaven (Revelation 12:7-8).

Scripture indicates there are multiple heavens in the spiritual dimension:

Two Realms Sustain Us

I know a man in Christ who fourteen years ago—whether in the body I do not know, or out of the body I do not know, God knows—such a man was caught up to the third heaven (2 Corinthians 12:2).

We can assume that God created the spiritual heavens before He made the natural heavens with stars, moons, planets, and solar systems. The scriptural use of the word "heaven" and its plural form references dwelling places in this natural realm and in the spiritual realm.

The Spiritual Realm

The natural heavens are where the planets and solar systems exist. The spiritual heavens are where angels dwell. Yes, God created a life form to dwell in the heavens of the spirit realm—the angels. We are not told when or how God made them, but Scripture says that they are spirit beings who inhabit the eternal realm, not as children, but as servants of God.

> *For to which of the angels did He ever say, "You are my son, today have I begotten you"? "I will be a Father to him and he shall be a son to me"?* (Hebrews 1:5)

When Scripture speaks of angels, it uses one Hebrew word in the Old Testament and one Greek word in the New Testament. Both the Greek and Hebrew words literally mean "messenger." While these words are used to speak of angels, they are also used to refer to mankind.

The Hebrew word *mal'ak* is used to refer to spirit beings 111 times and to human beings 102 times. The Greek word *aggelos* refers to spirit beings 181 times and mankind 7 times.

Both mal'ak and aggelos refer to messengers, who were sometimes men and sometimes angelic spirits.

Throughout Scripture the primary reason the angels exist is to serve God as messengers. They are spoken of in Scripture as ministering spirits that speak for God, to convey His eternal views as well as temporal insights to mankind.

> *Then the angel of the LORD called to Abraham a second time from heaven, and said, "By Myself I have sworn, declares the LORD..."* (Genesis 22:15-16).

> *But to which of the angels...Are they not all ministering spirits, sent out to render service?* (Hebrews 1:13-14)

These angelic beings do as they are instructed and convey what God intends to communicate. They are sent to bring mankind inspiration and insight. They appear at times to help us comprehend spiritual concepts we can apply to our life. In their service to God, angels also appear to watch over us, protect us, and track or record our activity:

> *And I saw the dead, the great and the small, standing before the throne, and books were opened; and another book was opened, which is the book of life; and the dead were judged from the things which were written in the books, according to their deeds* (Revelation 20:12).

People who pass from this natural life are even spoken of as angels in heaven (spirit beings) because they have been released from the limitations of this natural realm (Matthew 22:30; Mark 12:25). So there are a few, if not many, spiritual dwelling places, habitations called heavens, that we can partake of.

While the angels are spirit beings that occupy the spirit realm, they can also interact with the natural realm. Angels function as spirit beings with a mission of service, to convey God's will.

Creation 101

Once God conceptualized the natural realm, He spoke it into existence. When God speaks from His eternal perspective, it is as good as done.

> *Declaring the end from the beginning, and from ancient times things which have not been done, saying, "My purpose will be established, and I will accomplish all My good pleasure"* (Isaiah 46:10).

> *So will My word be which goes forth from My mouth; it will not return to Me empty, without accomplishing what I desire, and without succeeding in the matter for which I sent it* (Isaiah 55:11).

When God speaks and declares a word, we can be sure it will become so. His spoken word goes forth from His eternal realm to cover all time, from its beginning to its completion. In the natural realm however, things are made and matured through the progression of time. While God's spoken word can create something in a moment of time, He generally works within the progression of time, to make it so.

An example is found in the Genesis account of creation (1:1-31). This account does not speak of the sun and moon until the fourth day, so the earth's 24-hour day and night cycle must not have been operating in the first three creative cycles.

The Hebrew word (yom) translated "day" in Genesis means "a sphere of time," and is not necessarily a 24-hour cycle. Genesis 2:4 even speaks of the six creative days as a day. Thus, the scriptural days of creation were periods of unknown time frames. This account is not about a developmental order but is really about creative processes and cycles.

Consider this: When God spoke the creative word, from His eternal perspective, the natural universe came into existence. The making process He used could have begun with slowing down a portion of eternity's energy, to create the bit of matter the Big Bang theory supposes. The Creator could have placed within this congealed matter all the design features of what would become the natural universe. God could have designed it so the energy in this congealed portion of eternity would eventually superheat and explode to begin the process of developing into the vast expanding universe we observe today.

The natural realm was creatively designed and then progressively made into many groups of interwoven systems—from the microscopic to the immense. Minute atoms form molecular structures that together make up our planet. Earth is one of several planets in our particular solar system. A combination of many solar systems form a galaxy, and many galaxies make up the vast natural universe.

Everything in the natural realm is an organized system of molecular arrangements (from sand pebbles to planets and solar systems, to man-made objects), which can be measured by height, width, and depth.

Take a couple of minutes to watch this short video on the relative size of planets and stars:

https://www.youtube.com/watch?v=HEheh1BH34Q

When we observe the vast size of the universe (and this is only what we have discovered so far), we can, as many scientific minds do, get so engulfed by its immensity that we begin to think we are insignificant. We do not want to fall into this fallacy.

The Natural Earth

After the heavens of the universe were in place, God proceeded to create the earth as the place where mankind, His special creation, would be birthed to grow and develop.

> *God created…the earth* (Genesis 1:1).

> *Then God said, "Let the waters below the heavens be gathered into one place, and let the dry land appear"; and it was so. God called the dry land earth, and the gathering of the waters He called seas; and God saw that it was good* (Genesis 1:9-10).

We know that water covers two thirds of the surface of the earth. God gave us such an abundant supply of water because of its importance in sustaining life. Scientists have not found any living organisms on earth that do not have at least some amount of water. Most living things are comprised of about 50% water, while man himself is about 75% water. Water is a universal solvent, which carries nutrients to every part of our body and also carries away waste.

Water is also vital to the proper functioning of the earth itself. Its presence helps maintain a balance in the earth's climate and stabilizes its tectonic plates. Without water, earth would be a barren desert.

Then God said, "Let the waters teem with swarms of living creatures, and let birds fly above the earth in the open expanse of the heavens." ... "Let the earth bring forth living creatures after their kind: cattle and creeping things and beasts of the earth after their kind"; and it was so... and God saw that it was good (Genesis 1:20-25).

Not only was everything God created good, there was a lot of it: There are about 1,250,000 identified species of animals. This includes 1,190,200 invertebrates, among them 950,000 insects, 70,000 mollusks, 40,000 crustaceans, and 130,200 others. Then there are about 58,800 identified vertebrates, including 29,300 fish, 5,743 amphibians, 8,240 reptiles, 9,800 birds, and 5,416 mammals.

As a comparison, almost 300,000 plant species are known. In addition, there are innumerable species of bacteria and archaea (microbes).

And God created each one of us as unique offspring: Our fingerprints are complicated enough that it is possible for them all to be different. There are enough different elements in fingerprints to make it almost impossible for two fingerprints to have identical arrangements, even in identical twins.

At the DNA level, all humans are 99.9% identical. Each person's unique identity comes from the 0.1%, or one thousandth, of our DNA that is different. While humans are alike in many ways, each of us is amazingly unique!

How awesome are the works of God! It is any wonder that it takes a lifetime to comprehend them?

Two Realms Interact

While the natural realm functions in an orderly fashion, disruptive activity can and does occur. Natural systems clash and cause damage. We know that our solar system is quite orderly, yet comets and meteorites collide and explosions take place. Closer to home, when a tree falls in a forest, it brings harm to whatever it hits. The interaction of wind and temperatures can produce tornadoes and hurricanes that bring destruction.

This cause and effect principle also produces voids. When light is absent, darkness appears to fill the void. Likewise, cold is the absence of heat. We tend to think of darkness, cold, and even evil as forces that fight the better values, but they really are not. These apparent contrasts are powerless "void fillers" that reveal an absence of something. When light comes, darkness is always dispelled. Heat always diminishes cold. Scripture says good overcomes evil (Romans 12:21).

Many perceived opposites are really voids. *See Appendix I: "Cold, Dark and Evil" on page 153.*

Sometimes we ask why bad things happen to good people. Many voids and damaging effects are caused by natural events, but some are the result of accidents and people's misbehavior. Our maturing growth is affected by our response to these difficulties. We tend to excuse ourselves and blame situations or someone else. However, such responses can hold us captive to the ill side effects and stunt our spiritual growth.

This planet was uniquely created to provide an atmosphere where we transition from being merely offspring of God to becoming His disciplined children and mature sons of God.

The God of Scripture inhabits the eternal realm. This Eternal Being created the natural realm as a place of progressing times and contained spaces, to birth His offspring into existence, and to develop them (us) into mature children.

While this realm is not His primary dwelling place, He is not restricted from interacting with you and me while we are on the earth.

Memorize: *What is man that You* [God] *take thought of him, and the son of man that You care for him?* Psalms 8:4

Questions to consider:

1. How big is your God?

2. What are some of the differences between the spiritual realm and the material realm?

3. Why did God create the material universe?

Chapter 2

Body and Spirit Link Us

One day, the Creator of the heavens and earth assembled all the animals together and said, "I want to hide something from the humans until they are ready to receive it. It's the knowledge that I have put my Spirit within them."

First, an eagle spoke up, "Give it to me, and I will fly with it to the moon." God responded, "No. One day men will go there and find it."

Then a whale said, "Let me take it to the depths of the sea." "No," said God. "They will dive into the abyss someday."

Next, a buffalo said, "I will bury it on the Great Plains." The Creator replied, "They'll carve into the earth and find it even there."

Finally, an old grandmother mole, who lives underground without working eyes, but who sees with spiritual eyes, said, "Hide it inside of them." So God said, "It's as good as done!"

—From a Sioux Parable http://nativeamericancreation-mythology.weebly.com/sioux-creation-myth.html

Humanity Begins

Humanity began in the mind of God as a desire to birth and parent children. He wanted offspring who would grow, develop, and mature under His parental guidance. This chapter examines our body and spirit as foundational links that connect each of us to two different realities: the created natural realm and the eternal spiritual realm.

After creating the natural universe and seeing it properly functioning within the eternal spirit realm, God began filling the planet with various life forms. This included animal and plant life to populate the dry land, to occupy the waters, and to fly in the air. The creation is quite wonderfully made!

Then God spoke and His creative word began the process of birthing and developing His human offspring. Scripture records our beginnings in a few places:

> *God said, "Let Us make man in Our image, according to Our likeness"…male and female He created* [initiated] *them* (Genesis 1:26-27).

> *Then the LORD God formed man of dust…and breathed into his nostrils…life; and man became a living being* [soul] (Genesis 2:7).

To make the first human, Scripture says three actions were involved. God formed a body from the natural, material realm and then He breathed (infused) a measure of His Spirit into the body. Once the components of the natural and spiri-

Body and Spirit Link Us

tual realms were blended together into a being, a soul emerged as the person became conscious of itself and its surroundings.

Then God took a rib from the first being and formed a second, a woman, so the two could relate and complement one another.

> *The LORD God caused a deep sleep to fall upon the man, and he slept...God fashioned into a woman the rib...* (Genesis 2:21-22).

Thus, Adam and Eve were creatively formed. Three interacting components (body, soul, and spirit) were intertwined in the first human and then transferred into the second. Every descendant of this first man and woman possess the same tri-fold make-up. The New Testament confirms these three basic parts of what we are as a being:

> *May the God of peace Himself sanctify you entirely; and may your spirit and soul and body be preserved complete...*(1 Thessalonians 5:23).

Our body and spirit are foundational to our existence. They came from the eternal and natural realms, to connect us to both realities. The activity of these two components provides the interaction that allows our soul to form. We illustrate the soul on top of a triangle on the next page because it came from God's creative blending of the body and spirit components.

While our body was made from the dust of the natural realm, our spirit came from the Spirit God. Oh yes, every person has spirit and it came from God!

Thus declares the LORD who…forms the spirit of man within him (Zechariah 12:1).

It is a spirit in man, and the breath of the Almighty gives them understanding (Job 32:8).

The spirit of man is the lamp of the LORD, searching all the innermost parts of his being (Proverbs 20:27. Also see Psalms 32:2).

Our body, soul, and spirit are intricate members of what we are as living beings. Our soul, however, is our personal consciousness: a blend of mind, will, and emotion. The will of our soul is placed at the top of the triangle because it is formed by the foundational activity of our mind and emotions. We examine the soul in greater detail in chapter three.

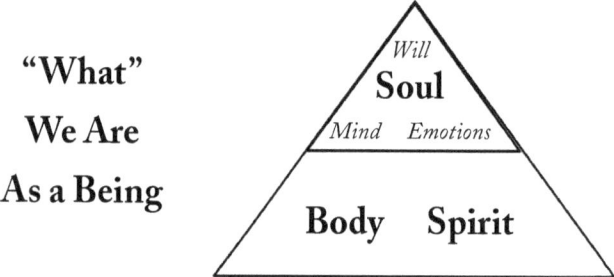

Our body, soul, and spirit can only partially be understood by examining them separately. To more fully comprehend them, we must see each part as interacting contributors to the functioning and welfare of our whole being. When we see and understand how our functional make-up, as a being, is a combination of these tri-fold components, we can then begin to appreciate the need, value, and function of each part.

Body and Spirit Link Us

What is our body without the spirit of life? How limited is the function of our body and spirit if our soul is immature? What if we didn't have emotions? What if our will did not function and give direction? Without each member of our make-up, our life would clearly be shortchanged.

Ongoing Process

After creating the first human, God began to clarify His relational intention by declaring that being alone is not good. Then He made the one into two—male and female—so mankind could participate in the ongoing process of birthing and raising His offspring. What a privilege we have to share in His creative undertaking!

> *God said, "It is not good for the man to be alone; I will make him a helper suitable…and they shall become one"* (Genesis 2:18, 24).

> *Now the man had relations with his wife Eve, and she conceived and gave birth to Cain, and she said, "I have gotten a manchild with the help of the LORD"* (Genesis 4:1).

God created the first man as the first step in a two-step process. Alone, Adam was incomplete. By creating a second person, God completed His initial intention of creating a relational "one." The one needed a complement to be complete. Scripture gives no indication the second was inferior to the first or that the first is not intended to complement the second. The two made a better one, a relational whole.

Both the man and the woman were important in setting up the ongoing process God had in mind from the beginning. He created and formed the first two so they and their offspring could relationally interact and assist Him in birthing and training the ongoing increase of His offspring. Yes, we are co-laborers with God in parenting His human children.

For we are God's fellow workers; you are God's field, God's building (1 Corinthians 3:9).

Every descendant of the first man and woman is the fruit of their union. Ever since the first couple, God births additional offspring into existence during the gestational process in their mother's womb. The spirit of life is at work in us from the day we are conceived, forming our beginnings.

You [God] *formed my inward parts; You wove me in my mother's womb...for I am fearfully and wonderfully made* (Psalm 139:13-14).

We are all offspring of our heavenly Father, through Adam and Eve. We all have a touch of God's life-giving Spirit within us because our human spirit came from God as an infusion (to permeate) of His Spirit.

It is good to realize there is a difference between offspring and children. In Scripture, offspring refers to those who live in various degrees of denial of God's fatherhood, while children refer to those who actively receive His parental guidance.

There was the true Light which, coming into the world, enlightens every man. He was in the world, and the world was made through Him, and the world did not know Him...as many as received Him, to them He gave the right to become children of God (John 1:9-12).

For it is for this we labor and strive, because we have fixed our hope on the living God, who is the Savior of all men, especially of believers (1 Timothy 4:10).

Links to Two Realms

Our body and spirit are foundational to our existence as humans. Scripture declares our body and our spirit came from different realms and each are destined to return to their source of origin.

Then the dust will return to the earth as it was, and the spirit will return to God who gave it (Ecclesiastes 12:7).

Do not trust in princes, in mortal man...His spirit departs, he returns to the earth. (Psalms 146:3).

Our body and spirit are actually two interwoven sides of our being. They link us to both realms of reality—the natural and the spiritual. Our body enables us to relate to, interact with, receive nutrition from, and be influenced by the natural realm and its inhabitants. Sounds simple enough!

What we often overlook is the fact that the spirit side of our being functions in much the same way as the body. Our human spirit enables us to relate to, interact with, receive nutrition from, and be influenced by the eternal spirit realm. This is also a simple reality, yet not always considered.

Our natural body cannot operate without proper care. When we neglect our body and fail to properly feed and exercise it, ill health limits our functioning and the quality of our life experience is greatly hampered. In like manner, when we neglect the spiritual side of our being and fail to feed and exercise our spirit, we shortchange the quality of our life.

We are physical and spiritual beings, even if we do not realize it or give ourselves to finding, experiencing, and maintaining full health for both parts. Actually, our body and spirit are so interwoven; it is often difficult to say that any one of our activities does not involve both.

> An Eskimo fisherman came to town every Saturday afternoon. He always brought his two dogs with him. One was white and the other was black. He had taught them to fight on command. Every Saturday afternoon in the town square the people would gather, and these two dogs would fight and the fisherman would take bets.
>
> On one Saturday the black dog would win; another Saturday, the white dog would win—but the fisherman always won! His friends began to ask him how he did it. He said, "I starve one and feed the other. The one I feed always wins because he is stronger."
> —*Billy Graham in* The Holy Spirit

We are natural and spiritual beings. While we learn to nurture, feed, clean, and take care of our body, we should also nurture, feed, clean, and take care of our spirit as well. Our overall health depends on it. And the interesting thing is we get to choose just how much we care for our self!

More than Natural

Even when we shy away from God or refuse to acknowledge Him, we are still related to Him as offspring. The deposit of God's Spirit gives each of us the potential to partake of more than a natural existence.

Body and Spirit Link Us

While science can inspect and measure our physical body, scientific technology cannot prove or disprove the reality of spirit. Science does, however, acknowledge things are going on in us they cannot explain. For instance, prayer has long been recognized as an influencing force that is beyond the ability of science to explain. There are many cases where miraculous recoveries occur, some with and some without medical treatment.

The spirit of life in each of us stirs a longing to partake of life beyond the natural time and space limitations. Our spirit inherently desires to interact with our eternal source of life and partake of our eternal purpose. Our spirit equips us to perceive and experience eternal realities. While our body is temporal, our spirit is an eternal part of what we are.

Throughout history, people have believed humans were comprised of a visible outer body and an inner, unseen self. While the outer body could be seen, they also perceived that we are much more than just a body. There is obviously an inner something that is able to direct our body's functioning. This unseen influence has been called our inner man. At times it is called our spirit, and at times it is spoken of as our soul.

The New Testament confirms the Old Testament creation account by declaring we have two unseen (non-physical) parts.

> *The Word of God is living…sharper than any two-edged sword, piercing as far as the division of soul and spirit* (Hebrews 2:12).

In the above verse, Scripture obviously declares our spirit and soul are not the same since they can be divided. But the actual difference remains a bit foggy to most of us. The difference becomes very clear in the next chapter.

The Apostle Paul acknowledged that we all came from a mutual source and that we are all offspring of God.

> *Men of Athens…while I was passing through and examining the objects of your worship, I also found an altar with this inscription, "TO AN UNKNOWN GOD." Therefore what you worship in ignorance, this I proclaim to you. The God who made the world and all things in it, since He is Lord of heaven and earth, does not dwell in temples made with hands…since He Himself gives to all people life and breath and all things; and He made from one man every nation of mankind to live on all the face of the earth…for in Him we live and move and exist, as even some of your own poets have said, "For we also are His children"* (Acts 17:22-28).

Every person is a combination of three different components, and the function of each contributes to the functioning of our whole being. We have an outer visible body and two unseen components—our human spirit and our conscious soul. Scripture is very clear: every person has a measure of God's Spirit as part of our basic human makeup.

While our body links us to the realities of the natural realm, our spirit links us to the realities of the spiritual realm and God Himself.

Five Natural Senses

We all have tools that help us make sense of our body and

Body and Spirit Link Us

spirit experiences. Our five senses help us observe and relate to both the natural and spiritual realities.

Our five physical senses of sight, smell, taste, touch and hearing assist our interaction in the natural environment. For example, our eyes sense light waves, our ears sense sound waves, while our nose senses tiny particles in the air. Our five natural senses are truly remarkable. Let's take a brief look at each of our natural senses.

Sight: The human eye is a truly amazing phenomenon. The eye is the medium which collects some 80% of the information received by its owner from the outside world. The tiny retina contains about 130 million rod-shaped cells, which detect light intensity and transmit impulses to the visual cortex of the brain by means of some one million nerve fibers.

The eyes can handle 500,000 messages simultaneously and are kept clear by ducts producing just the right amount of fluid with which the lids clean both eyes simultaneously.

Hearing: The human ear is composed of three main parts: the outer ear, the middle ear, and the inner ear. The outer ear is composed of the visible cartilage, the auditory canal, and the outer layer of the eardrum. The middle ear contains the hammer, anvil, and stirrup—the smallest bones in the human body.

The inner ear is where sound waves are converted to fluid waves, which in turn stimulate 30,000 hairs in the cochlea, a spiral like organ. The various frequencies are transmitted to the brain where they are processed and interpreted.

Taste: The gustatory system provides humans with the sense of taste. There are five main kinds of taste sensations: bitter, sour, salty, sweet, and savory. There are 8,000 to 10,000 taste buds on the human tongue, all of which are replaced about every two weeks.

Our human taste can serve as a warning system, which keeps us from ingesting harmful substances, or it can provide positive feedback on desirable delicacies.

Touch: The sense of touch can produce many different sensations such as hot, cold, pain, pleasure, smooth, rough, wet, dry, and so on. Five million nerve receptors are located on the surface of the skin, with additional sensors located internally. As with taste, the sense of touch can warn us of danger and it can also stir feelings of connectedness.

Smell: The human sense of smell is astonishing. Our sense of smell is located in the nasal cavity, which has over 40 million olfactory receptors. The receptors have tiny cilia projections that increase the area available to sense odors.

There are upwards of 1000 very specific odor receptors, and some people can differentiate about 2000 different odors. When we breathe or sniff, a chemical reaction takes place in the nose, which in turn transmit impulses to the olfactory cortex of the brain for interpretation.

Our five senses are amazing. They equip our physical body with unique senses that enable us to relate to and interact with each other and with the natural environment.

Our brain is amazing too in that it processes 100 million internal and environmental impulses per second. This allows us to process all these sensory perceptions simultaneously.

Five Spiritual Senses

Beyond the five natural senses we have just described, many speak of a sixth sense. The ability to sense something more than natural realities is often called ESP, which is short for Extrasensory Perception. Rather than having a similar sixth sense, Scripture reveals that our five senses have a spiritual side to their function.

Our spirit uses our five senses as tools to relate to and communicate with spiritual realities. Our unique ability to sense the natural realm may mirror our ability to sense spiritual realities. We are able to sense life beyond what our body is able to see, hear, taste, touch, and smell.

Our spirit's use of the five senses enables us to grasp what is hidden to our natural senses (I Peter 3:3-4). Scripture speaks more than a few times of the "heavens opening" so unnatural sights and perceptions can be seen and heard (2 Kings 6:13-16; Job 42:5; Isaiah 6; Daniel 6; Matthew 3:16-17; Acts 7:56; Acts 10:11; Revelation 1:9-12).

Jesus spoke of our use of the spiritual side of our senses as a means of receiving insightful direction from the Father of all spirits, just as He did.

> *The Son can do nothing of Himself, unless it is something He sees the Father doing; for whatever the Father does, these things the Son also does in like manner* (John 5:19).

The Apostle Paul said the exercise of our spiritual senses help us mature as children of God. Their function enables us to discern the presence of God and perceive the enlightening insights He shares.

> *Solid food is for the mature, who because of practice have their senses trained to discern good and evil* (Hebrews 5:14).

Let's look at a few of the Scriptures that speak of our spirit's use of our five senses to connect us to the spiritual realm.

Sight:

> *Now it came about in the thirtieth year…the heavens were opened and I saw visions of God* (Ezekiel 1:1).

> *He* [Stephen] *gazed intently into heaven and saw the glory of God…and he said, "Behold, I see the heavens opened up and the Son of Man standing at the right hand of God* (Acts 7:54-56).

> *But we all, with unveiled face, beholding as in a mirror the glory of the Lord, are being transformed into the same image from glory to glory* (2 Corinthians 3:18).

Hearing:

> *You came near and stood at the foot of the mountain… Then the LORD spoke to you from the midst of the fire; you heard the sound of words…He declared to you His covenant which He commanded you to perform, that is, the Ten Commandments* (Deuteronomy 4:11-13).

> *Then He said, "Go out, and stand on the mountain before the LORD." And behold, the Lord passed by…a great and strong wind…an earthquake…a fire…and after the fire a still small voice* (1 Kings 19:11-12 KJV).

> *But who has stood in the council of the LORD, that he should see and hear His word? Who has given heed to His word and listened?* (Jeremiah 23:18)

Taste:

> *O taste and see that the LORD is good* (Psalm 34:8).
>
> *How sweet are Your words to my taste! Yes, sweeter than honey to my mouth!* (Psalms 119:103).
>
> *Your words were found and I ate them, and Your words became for me a joy and the delight of my heart; for I have been called by Your name* (Jeremiah 15:16).
>
> *Like newborn babies, long for the pure milk of the word, so that by it you may grow in respect to salvation, if you have tasted the kindness of the Lord* (1 Peter 2:1-3).

Touch:

> *Then the LORD said to Moses, "Stretch out your hand toward the sky, that there may be darkness over the land of Egypt, even a darkness which may be felt"* (Exodus 10:21).
>
> *Everyone kept feeling a sense of awe; and many wonders and signs were taking place through the apostles* (Acts 2:43).

Smell:

> *But thanks be to God, who always leads us in triumph in Christ, and manifests through us the sweet aroma of the knowledge of Him in every place* (2 Corinthians 2:14).

We want to realize that we sense spiritual realities more often than we realize. When we observe a person's character, attitude, or personality, we are not observing them with our natural eyesight. These expressive features are perceived by the senses of our spirit. When a person has a near death experience, they do not observe what they see with physical senses. In another example, the feeling of love that we experience begins with the exercise of our spiritual senses.

The exercise of our five senses adds tremendous value to our life. The combination of both the natural and spiritual sides of our senses enhances our interaction with each other and enables us to experience deeper levels of relationship.

We are, indeed, created and made to relate! We are all designed to be aware of and be active in both the natural and spiritual realities. While we appear to be somewhat limited by our natural senses, we are not restricted to them.

Dominance

Our life begins with our five senses responding to our physical needs and desires, as we learn to relate to the variables of the natural realm. Scripture verifies our natural awareness and understandings are appropriate first experiences.

> *The spiritual is not first, but the natural; then the spiritual…*(1 Corinthians 15:46).

The first part of our developing awareness deals with the natural side of life. We learn how to eat, walk, relate, dress ourselves, etc. What we tend to overlook is the fact that from our first days, our spiritual senses are also being exercised. We learn to respond to spiritual realities like love and patience. Without realizing it, we experience and grow in many spiritual qualities. Scripture gives us a small list of these qualities:

> *But the fruit of the Spirit is love, joy, peace, patience,*

kindness, goodness, faithfulness, gentleness, self-control; against such things there is no law. If we live by the Spirit, let us also walk by the Spirit (Galatians 5:22-25).

Isn't it obvious that the fruits of the spirit listed above are more than natural characteristics with which we are born? These fruitful results are spiritual realities that we can partake of in this life. When we give ourselves to the practice of these spiritual qualities, life in this natural realm improves.

There are two Scriptures that address a contrast between our body and our spirit. These indicate, at first glance, that our body and spirit are rivals and competitors:

Walk by the Spirit, and you will not carry out the desire of the flesh. For the flesh sets its desire against the Spirit, and the Spirit against the flesh...for these are in opposition to one another, so that you may not do the things that you please (Galatians 5:16-17).

Those who are according to the flesh set their minds on the things of the flesh, but those who are according to the Spirit, the things of the Spirit...the mind set on the flesh is hostile toward God; for it does not subject itself [orderly submission] *to the law of God* (Romans 8:6-7).

These comparisons do not intend to indicate our body and spirit are rivals. Both passages simply provide cautions about setting our mind primarily on natural and physical desires which are called "fleshly."

Our body and our flesh are different! *See Appendix II: "Body and Flesh" on page 158.*

To the degree that we become spiritually aware and partake of our heavenly Father's guidance, so His Spirit becomes a prevailing influence over the natural side of our life. When we negate the value of our human spirit's interaction with the Spirit of God and with one another, we tend to limp through life and miss much of what we are designed to experience.

Our body is not bad and does not separate us from God or make us sin any more than our spirit makes us sinless and routinely in harmony with God. Nurturing and exercising both our body and spirit senses increases our overall quality of life, while ignoring either one limits our maturing process. When we interact with the presence of God, our spirit is fed and gains a God-ordained, guiding influence over our interactions.

All of us have a spirit within us, even if we do not realize it. This indwelling spirit of life gives each of us the ability to relate and communicate with the Father of all spirits and enables each of us to receive insightful thoughts and directions from God. As we will see in the coming chapters, the choice is ours to make!

Memorize: *"This is eternal life, that they may know You, the only true God, and Jesus Christ whom You have sent."* John 17:3

Questions to consider:

1. What are the three basic components that comprise every human?

2. What are the two realm links and sides of every human being?

3. Why is it important to recognize that we all have a functional spiritual side to our being, with spiritual senses?

Chapter 3

Conscious Soul Informs Us

Our soul is where we gather, evaluate, and act upon information flowing to us. Having information can be very valuable, but having useful information is indispensable:

A man in a hot air balloon realized he was lost. He reduced altitude and spotted a man below.

He descended a bit more and shouted, "Excuse me, can you help me? I promised a friend I would meet him an hour ago, but I don't know where I am."

The man below replied, "You are in a hot air balloon, hovering approximately 30 feet above the ground." Then he added, "You are between 40 and 41 degrees north and between 59 and 60 degrees west longitude."

"You are obviously a technical person," said the balloonist.

"I am," replied the man, "but how did you know?"

"Well," answered the balloonist, "everything you told me is technically correct, but I have no idea what to make of your information, and the fact is I am still lost. Frankly, you've not been much help to me at all."

The man below responded, "You must be in management."

"I am," replied the balloonist, "but how did you know?"

"Well," said the man, "you don't know where you are or where you are going. You have risen to where you are due to a large quantity of hot air. You made a promise, which you have no idea how to keep, and you expect people beneath you to solve your problems. The fact is you are in exactly the same position you were in before we met, but now, somehow, it's my fault."

This chapter will help us understand what our soul is, how it develops, how it functions, and what factors influence the decisions we make in life. We shall see that our soul is the combined activity of our mind, will, and emotions: our ability to consciously register what we experience.

Soul Becomes

As we have seen, God created the first human by combining elements from the natural and spiritual realms into a living being. Every one of us originates from this formative beginning. We all have a body and spirit that link us to both the natural and spiritual realities. While our body and spirit connects us to our realms of origin, our five senses are the tools we use to relate with both of these realms.

Mankind's existence began in the earth as a lump of clay when God fused a touch of His eternal Spirit into the formed body, a heart began to beat, a soul started to exist, and a personal consciousness emerged.

When the soul of the first man came into existence, it rapidly began to record information and form perceptions of reality. The soul provides a personal awareness of self, of others, of the world around us and enables us to interact with our creative Father.

The word "soul" speaks of our ability to register into a personal consciousness what we sense and experience. This third component in "what" we are as a human being is a blend of the activity of our mind, will, and emotion.

Our **Mind** is the part of our conscious awareness that thinks, reasons, and compares.

Our **Will** is the part of our conscious awareness that understands, forms beliefs, and decides.

Our **Emotion** is the part of our conscious awareness that feels, desires, and is passionate.

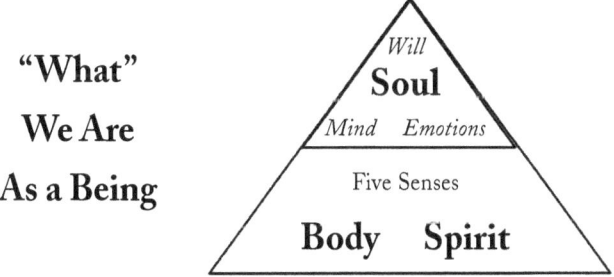

"What"
We Are
As a Being

In the same way that our body and spirit activity are foundational to the formation of our soul, our mind and emotion activity are foundational to the formation of our will.

Our consciousness blends what our mind thinks and our emotion feels, into what our will understands. Our personal perception of truth and reality emerges and develops as we become consciously aware of the reality that exists in both the temporal and eternal realms.

Influencing Factors

A simple example will illustrate how these three attributes of our soul function together: Bill walks into a car dealership to buy a car. He looks at the various models in the showroom and is drawn to the red convertible. He imagines himself driving down the road enjoying his new purchase and the admiring looks the car brings (emotion). Then he walks over to a white minivan and remembers (mind) he has four kids and a wife. In this case, his mind's reasoning wins out over his emotional response to the convertible. He decides to buy the minivan (will).

Our mind and emotion are constantly registering the experiences of our physical and spiritual senses. Then the reasoning of our mind and the feelings of our emotion formulate our understanding and determine our course of action.

Although our perceptions are not always complete or correct, we tend to believe our conclusions, be they: I am beautiful or ugly; I am strong or weak; I am valuable or worthless; I am loved or despised. What we understand about ourselves has a huge impact on the quality of the life we live.

Conscious Soul Informs Us

Everything we perceive and come to understand about ourselves, God, and life in general forms our will. In turn, our will influences how we further think and feel about our additional life experiences. Our journey through life is guided by our formed and re-formed understandings.

The importance of our emotion is often overlooked or discounted. At times we are told, "Your emotion/feelings cannot be trusted." Other times we hear, "Go with your gut feelings." God made our emotion as a support for our soul consciousness. Just because we are able to formulate what we think into words and have difficulty describing our feelings, we should not assume our ability to reason is more important than our emotion. God has endowed us with emotion, and we want to recognize it is a valuable and equalizing asset of our soul.

There are times when feelings can be a greater motivator than reason. The emotion of a moment can cause someone to ignore reason and become a hero in a dangerous situation. Feelings can easily be a strengthening influence in our relationships with each other. What we feel when we apply ourselves to a task will most always affect the quality of the outcome. A show of emotion can quickly verify a conviction regarding an issue and a relationship.

When we submit our conscious soul (what we think, feel, and believe) to our heavenly Father's input, our soul experiences what Scripture calls a renewing of the spirit of our mind.

> *...that you be renewed in the spirit of your mind, and put on the new self, which in the likeness of God has been created (although not fully formed) in righteousness and holiness of the truth* (Ephesians 4:23-24).

When we respond to God's guidance, we mature at a greater rate into our Father's image and likeness. As we receive our Father's insight and follow His guidance, we are able to partake of an eternal quality of life right here on earth:

This is eternal life, that they may know You, the only true God, and Jesus Christ whom You have sent (John 17:3).

Finally, brethren, whatever is true, whatever is honorable, whatever is right, whatever is pure, whatever is lovely, whatever is of good repute, if there is any excellence and if anything worthy of praise, dwell on these things (Philippians 4:8).

It is often said: "You are what you eat," and "You are what you think." Both of these maxims are true. We become what our spirit and flesh consume, as well as what our soul consciously thinks, feels, and comes to believe. Our soul is continually collecting and evaluating information from our experiences and from what we reflect on or meditate about.

Our spiritual senses are active every day, even though we do not realize it. The activity of our spirit is unseen by the natural eye, but the eye of our spirit does observe. These observations enable us to consciously become aware of non-physical realities such as love.

Our conscious soul draws not only from our natural activities; it draws from our spiritual activity as well. These interactions formulate our perception of what is real into a personal understanding of reality. Here are two questions we can ask ourselves: Just who are we becoming? Is who we are becoming intentional?

Conscious Soul Informs Us

A Team

To fully comprehend how our soul functions, we must view all contributing parts as interwoven members. Our soul is more than a haphazard collection of what we think, feel, or understand—it's a fusion of all three. The commitments our will chooses to make are only as stable as the support received from our reasoning mind and feeling emotion.

Consider these three examples:

When Joe and Ericka first saw each other, they were immediately smitten. Both were physically attracted to each other and emotional sparks flew, indicating they were meant for each other. It felt right and within minutes they decided this was a relationship meant to last. Joe and Ericka chose to pursue a close relationship based on their feelings. However, they soon discovered they had very few common interests. After three months when supporting reason fell short, it became obvious that feelings were not enough to sustain a long-term relationship. Later, gator!

Six months later this same Joe met Katie and again sparks began to fly. Both of them felt this was it! Following a few dates, they discovered they had many things in common. It became clear to Joe that things were different this time because their compatibility supported their feelings. Eventually Joe and Katie solidified their relationship in marriage. Happily ever after!

In the meantime, Ericka visited a muscum with a friend. The friend spotted an acquaintance and introduced Ericka to John. After a little conversation that revealed similar interests, they decided to get better acquainted. After a few dates

Ericka and John realized the chemistry was missing. Without the emotional attraction, they decided to not pursue the relationship. Adios!

In the first scenario, Joe and Ericka pursued a relationship that was based on an agreement between their feelings (emotion) and choice (will). This was eventually sabotaged by a lack of common interests (reason). In the second scenario, Joe chose to start a relationship with Katie based on feelings, but this time compatible interests were a support that strengthened their commitment. In the third scenario, Ericka and John chose to pursue a relationship based on common interests, but it ended when it became obvious the emotional attraction was missing.

A three-fold agreement between our mind, will, and emotion is essential for lasting stability in any commitment. Scripture verifies this truth:

> *And if one can overpower him who is alone, two can resist him. A cord of three strands is not quickly torn apart.* (Ecclesiastes 4:12).

The soul team is a combination of our mind, will, and emotion. Together, they hold us to consciously relate and make commitments. They allow us to relate to spiritual realities like God, angels, and the insights God reveals for our life.

This team-like principle facilitates all our commitments. For instance, when a marriage becomes difficult, feelings may wane and reasons for separation can begin to accumulate. When this happens, we can choose to restore the failing relationship by reviving the weakening feelings and renewing reasons for the relationship. This three-fold factor is an influencing feature in all relationships.

Ingrained Preferences

Each of our physical and spiritual experiences stimulates our soul to think, feel, and develop personal perceptions. What we come to understand, in turn, sways and influences how we further think and feel about life, our relationships, and additional experiences. When our body touches a hot surface, what we think and feel forms an understanding to help us avoid the hot surface in the future.

As a child, the first time I ate cow's liver, my sense of taste and smell found it offensive and I got physically sick. The experience caused me to feel and reason (emotion and mind) that liver was not good for me. This understanding influenced me for many years. When I smelled or heard liver was going to be served, my memories influenced my mind and emotion with the apprehension "You are in trouble." My body reacted to the directional insight and I would begin to get physically sick.

This same conscious flow happens when our human spirit interacts with the spirit realm. When we sense the love of God sweep over us, or a conviction grips us, it is our spirit that is sensing God's influential and insightful presence.

> *Everyone whose heart stirred him and everyone whose spirit moved him came and brought the LORD'S contribution for the work of the tent of meeting and for all its service and for the holy garments* (Exodus 35:21).

> *When Jesus therefore saw her weeping, and the Jews who came with her also weeping, He was deeply moved in spirit and was troubled* (John 11:33).

The thoughts and feelings generated by the Spirit of God and the spirit in others can influence our perceptions. What we understand then sways our reactions to influence the way we conduct ourselves.

While the activities of our body and spirit stir both thoughts and feelings in us, we are generally more responsive to one or the other. In other words, we all tend to be more responsive to either mental or emotional stimulation. For instance, if our inclination is stronger toward mental stimulus, we are inspired more by the reasoning in a presentation: like the facts or the words of a song. If our tendency is toward emotional stimuli, we are inspired more by the feeling we get from the presentation: like the emotional stories or the music of a song. The least dominant part of our soul will then either contrast or complement the stronger one.

Our thoughts and feelings also influence each other. What we reason may cause us to feel a certain situation or insight is acceptable. On the other hand, an uneasy feeling can cause us to think the situation or insight is off. Our reasoning mind can override an emotional feeling in the same way a strong emotional feeling can override a reasoning mind.

What we reason and feel influences what we believe about everything. When we say "I like or dislike," "I will or cannot," "I agree or disagree," we express the perceptions and understanding of our will.

Conscious Soul Informs Us

Our family heritage can greatly influence and help form our thoughts, attitudes, and the habits we develop. Additional influencing factors can come from the environment we currently live in and from previous choices we've made.

Joe grew up in a home where there was a lot of love, which spilled over into the neighborhood. His home was a place of refuge for many of the neighborhood kids.

Less than two blocks away lived a very different family. John grew up with constant bickering, an occasional fist fight, and eventually drug use. The police were called in from time to time to settle domestic disputes. With all this dysfunction, the youngest family members were caught up in an unending cycle of destruction.

It can take a good bit of insight and determination to overcome the negative influences we grow up with. On the other hand, positive family influences can stay with us for the rest of our lives.

What we understand formulates our perception of reality. *See Appendix III: "Get Understanding" on page 163.*

Will's Choice

Our heavenly Father gives freedom of choice to each of His offspring. The ability to choose is commonly called "free will" because it is an attribute of our will.

The understandings of our will, be they right or wrong, tend to rule over the activity of our mind and emotion, which then gives influencing direction to our actions. If I believe God does not exist, I will not consider the insights He shares with me. If I believe you are my enemy, I will tend to treat you with suspicion. If I have learned to forgive, as Christ did on the cross, I will not take offense. When I chose to be like or unlike my parents, it's an exercise of my will, which is then supported by my thoughts and feelings.

During our human beginnings, the first couple chose to believe a deception about God's will for us. They embraced the idea that instead of living as dependent children of God, they could live independent of Him and be "as God." When Adam and Eve exercised their will and chose to separate from God's guidance, their choice sent them and their offspring into the deathly destructive lifestyles we still deal with today.

Ill-conceived responses to God usually result in troublesome lives. Cain refused God's instruction and his life turned sour (Genesis 4:1-16). King Saul did whatever he wanted and his kingdom was given to another (1Samuel 13:13-14). The wife of King David's youth despised his unreserved worship of God and the next king of Israel was mothered by a different woman (2 Samuel 6:16-23).

When we exercise our will and choose to make a commitment, be it in marriage, to a specific job, toward a health benefit, or an active fellowship with God, it is usually because a mental or an emotional stimulus has influenced our will to agree. For our commitments to endure, we need the full support of our mental reasoning and our emotional feeling.

We really do have a choice in how we live. As young adults we can choose whether we are going to be governed by the concepts we were raised with or alter them.

Conscious Soul Informs Us

While we may be limited by our natural senses, we are not restricted to them. The Bible shares stories of successful people who listened to God. Enoch walked with God and didn't fall victim to the errors of his day. Noah responded to God's direction and his whole family was saved from the destruction of the Flood. Abraham heard God and willingly responded to become as a father to the faithful.

Moses, with all his insecurities and faults, became a friend of God. Moses came to believe in the power of God by observing His miraculous activity.

> *O LORD God, You have begun to show Your servant Your greatness and Your strong hand; for what god is there in heaven or on earth who can do such works and mighty acts as Yours?* (Deuteronomy 3:24)

Anytime the unlimited ability of the eternal God is compared with the created natural realm, we are amazed at the difference. Unfortunately, even though we become aware of spiritual realities, too often we fail to give them enough consideration.

During Moses' day, Israel refused to hear God speak to them personally and then was unwilling to believe what He said to Moses. Nevertheless, God's heart toward them remained faithful; even in their unfaithfulness He still cared for them. For 40 years their clothes didn't wear out; they continued to eat manna and quail and drink water from a rock! That generation remained in the wilderness and eventually died there. God is faithful even when we are not. Our unwillingness to relate, however, affects how much we partake of God's grace.

Choose for yourselves today whom you will serve…but as for me and my house, we will serve the LORD (Joshua 24:15).

Soul's Salvation

We want to realize that the ill results of bad decisions can be reversed or at least amended as our responses to God change and improve. David was a man "after God's own heart" and was God's anointed king, yet he committed adultery and murder. When David repented, he was able to again receive God's full favor. David went on to declare:

Create in me a clean heart, O God, and renew a steadfast spirit within me (Psalm 51:9-10).

We want to also be aware that our good reactions to God's guidance are not a guarantee that our response will be good every time. Responsive people can still turn away from God's ways and begin to walk in the way of destruction for a moment or for an extended period of time.

But if the wicked man turns from all his sins which he has committed and observes all My statutes and practices justice and righteousness, he shall surely live…But when a righteous man turns away from his righteousness, commits iniquity and does according to all the abominations that a wicked man does, will he live? (Ezekiel 18:21, 24)

As we realize the contributing value our thoughts and feelings have on the development of our will, we can be more discerning of the things we dwell on and entertain. After all, who we are and are becoming depends a lot on it.

When our first parents chose to ignore God's guidance, they

Conscious Soul Informs Us

began living separate from God. Scripture tells us they even tried to hide from God's presence (Genesis 3:8). The separation clouded their ability to clearly understand their Father. Their choice to self-rule also resulted in their separation from the Tree of Life (Genesis 3:8-23).

Our positive response to God's guiding presence begins to reverse the blinding influence we inherit from our first parents' separation. As we give ourselves to God's guidance, we experience times of refreshing (Acts 3:19), redemption (Romans 3:23-24), and the salvation of our soul.

> *Therefore, putting aside all filthiness and all that remains of wickedness, in humility receive the word implanted, which is able to save your souls* (James 1:21).

I became aware of God's presence during my pre-teen years and committed my life to pursuing His will. As a teenager I often worked the dinner shift in a local restaurant. One evening while walking to work, I remembered some of the conversion stories I'd recently heard and began to wonder if I was missing out on something important. Conversion stories usually tell of graphic experiences people have when they turn to God. I asked God if I should walk away from His fellowship so I could have a conversion experience. I immediately sensed God say, "You have chosen the better way."

We can make a commitment to God without a dramatic conversion event. We can become aware of God and learn early on to follow His guiding insights as a child. We can excrcise our will and decide to respond to God's input as a young person or a mature adult. Our eternal Father is always available for our receptive response to His guidance.

Our soul is always observing, absorbing, and reacting to our body and spirit experiences. Our soul then interprets our experiences as perceptions about both natural and spiritual realities. As we respond to our heavenly Father's guiding insight, we learn to think and feel as God thinks and feels about our life purpose.

Every commitment requires our soul's full agreement (mind, will, and emotion) before they can become a habitual guide to our actions. Once we perceive new insight regarding the health of our body, soul, or spirit, a process is needed to develop and establish our understanding.

Science tells us that when we entertain new thoughts, our physical brain begins to create new neurological pathways. It takes 21 days for a new thought pattern to establish new pathways. Then the old neurological pathways that we no longer use begin to die out. If we revert back to old thoughts, we keep them alive as options. Our new perceptions must become established understanding before they fully influence our actions. (http://www.stevenaitchison.co.uk/blog/a-new-habit/)

When we begin to understand that a relational fellowship with God is healthy, we must choose to give ourselves to active interaction. We do this by reading Scripture, by spending time with like-minded people, and by entertaining His insightful presence. A casual commitment will obviously not bring the best results.

Since our soul plays a major role in the activity of our body and spirit, it is a major factor in what we are and who we become. It is our soul that develops an awareness of ourselves

Conscious Soul Informs Us

and other people, interprets the world around us, and accepts or rejects greater insight.

Scripture encourages us with these words:

> *My righteous one shall live by faith; and if he shrinks back, my soul has no pleasure in him. But we are not of those who shrink back to destruction, but of those who have faith to the preserving of the soul* (Hebrews 10:38-39).
>
> *…in humility receive the word implanted, which is able to save your souls* (James 1:21).
>
> *…obtaining as the outcome of your faith the salvation of your souls* (1 Peter 1:8-9).
>
> *Incline your ear and come to Me. Listen, that you* [literally your soul] *may live* (Isaiah 55:3).
>
> *So then…work out your salvation…for it is God who is at work in you, both to will and to work for His good pleasure* (Philippians 2:12-13).

Every person has the potential to grow up in all respects and mature as a child of God. We want to stay faithful to the maturing development of what we think, feel, and believe.

The salvation of our soul is what God is after. At death, our spirit returns to Him and our body returns to the earth. The question is what about our soul consciousness. In truth, our soul is more connected to our spirit than our body, and it enters the eternal realm. The real question is: In what condition does our consciousness enter the eternal realm?

As our soul matures under God's guidance, we become more

than the love of His heart, we can become the apple of His eye as developing children (Zechariah 2:8) and the delight of His heart (Psalms 16:3).

Memorize: *"Therefore, putting aside all filthiness and all that remains of wickedness, in humility receive the word implanted, which is able to save your souls."* James 1:21

Questions to consider:

1. Our soul consciousness is a blend of what three functions?

2. How is our personal belief system formed?

3. What part of our being needs to be reconciled to God and each other?

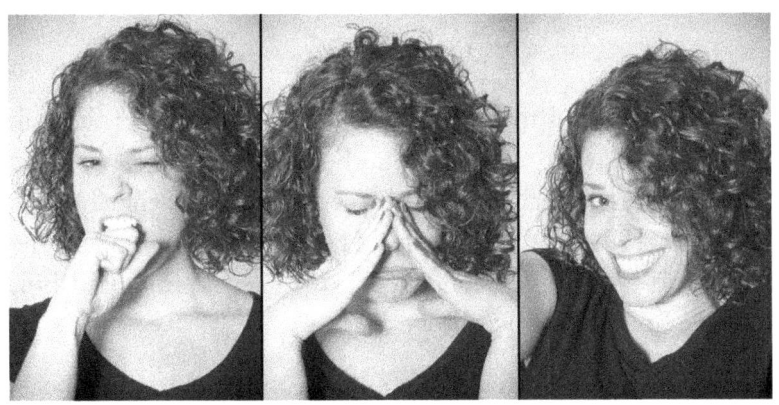

Chapter 4

Expressive Heart Reveals Us

He was one of five siblings, born to a construction worker and homemaker. They lived in the deep South and one of his first jobs was working for a plumbing contractor. At age 16 John said of it, "I never drew inspiration from that miserable work." His heart was not in it.

When he was halfway through college, he worked part time in retail sales as a sales clerk in the men's underwear section of a department store, which he described as a "humiliating" experience. His heart was not in that either.

After completing college and earning a law degree, he had intended to pursue a career as a tax lawyer. He was soon overcome by the "complexity and lunacy" of it. His heart was not in that profession either so he returned to his hometown to become a trial lawyer.

After a decade of practicing law and serving in his state legislature, he decided to try his hand at writing a novel. It took him three years to complete the book, but these three years were different because his heart was finally in what he was doing. In 1991 he turned once again to the writing he so enjoyed and began his second novel. Its success prompted him to leave his law practice altogether.

In each of the years that followed, he continued to write bestselling novels. Why? Because he finally found his heart's true expression. Who is this well-known novelist? You may have heard of him: John Grisham, author of *The Firm, The Pelican Brief, The Client*, and many others. It seems that when a person's heart is in their work, they can be very successful!

The Real You

Mankind began as a thoughtful desire in God. After creating the natural universe, He formed a body from the natural realm and fused a touch of His eternal Spirit into the body. As the being began to animate and live, a consciousness (soul) began to develop.

This relational composite of body, soul, and spirit equips each of us with a unique ability to partake of and interact with both the natural and spiritual realms. God has gifted each of us with the ability to express ourselves as a means of dealing with our built-in need to connect with and relate to the Spirit of God and to one another.

While our body, soul, and spirit describe what we are as a being, our heart defines who we are as a person. It will become apparent through this chapter that our heart represents who we are—the real us.

Expressive Heart Reveals Us

We initially think of our heart as an organ located in the center of our body. While our physical heart is central to our function as a human being, scripturally speaking, our heart represents something more.

> *Man looks at the outward* [natural] *appearance, but the LORD looks at the heart* (1 Samuel 16:7).

If our heart is what God observes, then we want to understand what God considers our heart to be, so we can give it suitable attention.

Everyone tends to associate our heart with our deepest feelings as well as what we really think about issues. We often hear phrases like, "His heart is not in it" and "You should follow your heart." These common phrases show that we all sense our heart is more than just a physical organ.

At first glance, Scripture appears to confuse an understanding of heart because it associates the heart of man with nearly every part of what we are. Pick up any Bible concordance and skim through the verses that speak of the heart. You will find our heart is associated with our soul's mind, will, and emotion as well as the five senses of our body and spirit.

Here's a small sampling of scriptures to illustrate the point: The heart can be meek (Matthew 11:29), pure (Matthew 5:8), glad (Isaiah 65:14), hard (Mark 3:5), proud (Psalm 101:5), troubled (John 14:1), fearful (John 14:27), trusting (Proverbs 3:5), forgiving (Matthew 18:35), circumcised (Deuteronomy 30:6), angry (Ecclesiastes 7:9), and renewed (Ezekiel 18:30-32). The list can go on and on.

A few years ago, as I reviewed the insights I'd received about the functional relationship between our body, soul, and spirit, I began to wonder just how the heart of man fits into the picture. Does our heart belong in the center of our what triangle or, as many assume, is it our spirit or maybe our soul? So I asked God, "Where does our heart fit into this picture? Lord, how do You define the heart of man?"

"Who"—Our Added Value

As I reexamined Scripture's use of "heart," insight came. I began to realize our heart is not our spirit or our soul, even though it is linked to each of these components, nor is our heart defined as one or all of our five senses. It became clear that God defines our heart as the expression that springs from our whole being—body, soul, and spirit.

Ancient Greek scholars believed that everything is the sum total of its parts, and a description of the parts adequately describes the thing. This formula, however, fails to consider the added value that is created by function. When parts are assembled and function as a unit, they create something that adds tremendous value beyond the sum of its parts.

For example, when lamp parts are assembled and function as a unit, light is produced, which is a much greater value than simply a pile of wires, bulbs, and bases. Similarly, when complex airplane parts are assembled as a unit, they can produce the added value of flight.

When God combined the body, soul, and spirit components into the first human being, He created us as functioning units. The function of our collective parts produces the added value of expression. This added value is our expressive heart.

Expressive Heart Reveals Us

A close examination of Scripture clarifies our heart is our expressive self, which springs from our entire being.

The general confusion about heart is a hold-over from the historical perception that we are a two-part being—one visible and one invisible. As we have seen in chapter three, we have two unseen components— our spirit and our soul.

> *For the word of God is living and active and sharper than any two-edged sword, and piercing as far as the division of soul and spirit, of both joints and marrow, and able to judge the thoughts and intentions of the heart* (Hebrews 4:12).

Our heart is closely connected to every aspect of what we are as a being because it is the added value produced by the function of our collective components. Our heart creates who we are as a person. Our heart displays godly or ungodly values in everything we say and do.

> *My son, give attention to my words; incline your ear to my sayings. Do not let them depart from your sight; keep them in the midst of your heart. For they are life to those who find them and health to all their body. Watch over your heart with all diligence, for from it flow the springs of life* (Proverbs 4:20-23).

While our expressive heart is involved in everything we say and do, our heart infuses the quality of values we possess into each of our actions. God appears to consider the quality of our expressions, our heart values, to be the most significant aspect of our life experience:

> *I, the LORD, search the heart...even to give to each man according to his ways* [expressive activity] (Jeremiah 17:10).
>
> *Search me, O God, and know my heart; try me...and lead me in the everlasting way* [godly activity] (Psalm 139:23-24).
>
> *He* [God] *also testified and said, "I have found David... a man after my heart, who will do all My will"* (Acts 13:22).
>
> *Let no unwholesome word proceed from your mouth, but only such a word as is good for edification according to the need of the moment, so that it will give grace to those who hear* (Ephesians 4:29).

Scripture makes it clear that God looks beyond our composite make up to consider the quality of our expressive activity. If this is how God sees us, then we want to become more aware of our response to His guidance.

Projected Persona

The dictionary defines persona as: "a person's perceived or evident disposition; personal image; public role." Persona is another way of identifying the added value that is produced by the collective functioning of our body, soul, and spirit.

Persona is our expressive heart. The expressions that come from us disclose our persona, our personhood, who we are as an individual person. When somebody asks, "Who are you?" or "Whom did you see?" we automatically assume a body with spirit and soul is involved. These queries seek a name and details to reveal a specific persona.

Expressive Heart Reveals Us

While the expressions of our heart are partially revealed to the physical eye, it is the eye of our spirit that enables us to observe such expressive realities as character, attitude, and personality. Since everyone has spiritual senses, we can all see one another's heart expression, even though we do not always understand what we see and perceive. Heart reveals our unique significance as an individual person, who we are.

The features we project as expressions are categorized as character, attitude, and personality, or CAP. These expressive features help define our heart and allow us to view and understand who we are as a person.

God created us as functional beings that radiate with expression. When you say someone's name, for example Suzy, an image pops up in your mind that includes how Suzy expresses herself and how she communicates, not just what she looks like or what she does for a living.

We often confuse our occupations or achievements (what we do) with our identity (who we are). One of the first questions that comes up in conversations is, "What do you do for a living?" to which we honestly answer, "I'm a doctor," or "I'm a minister," or "I'm retired." But this only scratches the surface. These answers are about what we do, not who we are. Other typical questions that arise are, "Where do you work?" "Do you have kids?" "Where do you live?" Again, these are questions that ask about the details of our lives and not who we are as a person.

KEY POINT: Our occupation is not our identity; our ministry is not our identity; nor is our family status our identity. What we do or have is not who we are. Our value as a person does not depend on these things! We are much more than what we are and do as a being.

A pastor once suggested that we answer the occupation question like this, "I'm a follower of Christ who does _____." This answer puts the emphasis on who we are relationally and not on what we do. Our jobs and situations may change, but our persona continues with us into the next job and situation. How about answering like this, "I'm a loving husband and devoted father who is employed as a _____." Or, "I'm a student of life who attends _____ College."

Our persona demonstrates our values as the person we have become and illustrates the quality of our heart. This is why after some dramatic situation happens, we sometimes hear, "I didn't realize he was that kind of person."

Expressive Countenance

We all respond to situations and circumstances with a countenance, an appearance that displays our heart for all to see. When someone says, "I see God in you," the eye of their spirit is observing a character, attitude, or personality (CAP) trait of God that we are projecting.

The quality of our expressions can identify us as having the heart of a father or mother, having either a caring or calculating heart, or having either a servant's or a selfish heart. The quality of our expressive countenance can indicate that we are or are not a godly person.

To illustrate our expressive heart as our persona, relating who we are as a person to what we are as a being, it would look like this:

Expressive Heart Reveals Us

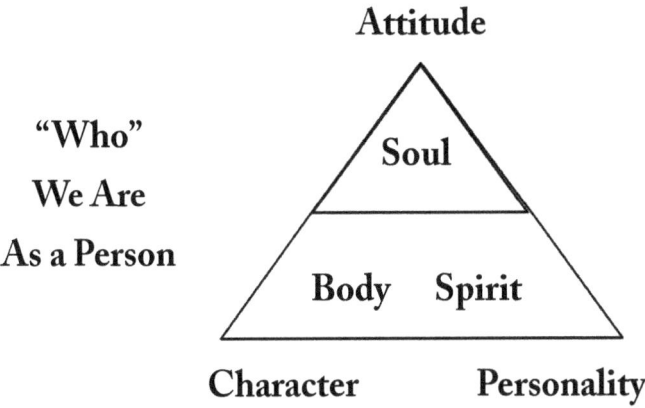

Again, the expressive features that project *who* we are as a person are described as character, attitude, and personality (CAP). When we flip the triangle to visualize CAP as the expressive features of our heart, we may be able to better understand. Just remember, attitude is our heart's crowning feature.

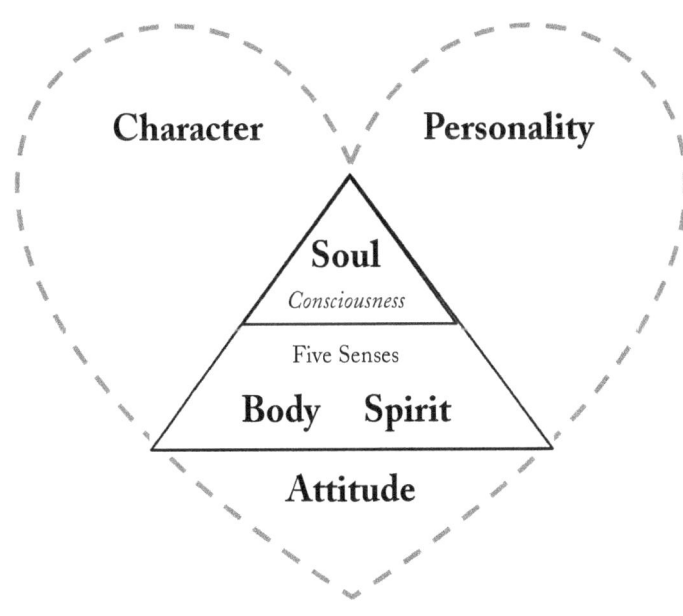

Let's put this into context. What we are as a being is not who we are as a person. It is the function of our what components that produce the added expressive value of heart. Our heart expression illustrates who we are as a person and provides a context for defining our real self.

The way we relate to one another is based on the values and qualities we illustrate in our CAP expressions. As we will examine in detail in chapter five, God created us to become reflections and resemblances of His heart. Our expressions are what glorifies or dishonors God.

> *The things that proceed out of the mouth come from the heart and those defile the man* (Matthew 15:18).

CAP Expressions Define Us

We want to visualize our heart not so much as something that is in us, but as the expression that emanates from us. Let's take a few minutes to describe each CAP feature of our heart. Each one is quite different.

Character traits speak of our dominant moral fiber—such as: honest or deceitful, kind or mean, loyal or shifty, charitable or selfish.

Attitude traits speak of our temperament—such as: loving or hateful, humble or proud, flexible or rigid.

Personality traits speak of our social behavior—such as: analytical, supportive, organized, or outgoing.

Each feature of our CAP, our relational persona, is worth a closer look.

Expressive Heart Reveals Us

Character—Moral Fiber

Character is the expression of our heart that demonstrates our moral fiber. The dictionary defines character as: "the aggregate of features and traits that form the individual nature of a person; moral or ethical quality; qualities of honesty, courage, or the like; integrity."

Although most people's moral character fails to be good or bad all the time and in every situation, we do tend to be more one than the other. We all lean toward being respectful, trustworthy, responsible, kind, fair, and caring, or not. Most everyone has a few good characteristics.

Let's look at one heart expression—kindheartedness—and see how it can be manifested. This was vividly depicted by a character in an old TV series called "The Waltons," which was based on the book, Spencer's Mountain. The story is set in rural Virginia during the Great Depression and WWII. The patriarch of the family, John Walton Sr., was characterized as consistently being kindhearted. One episode shows John helping a neighbor family through a difficult situation.

The fictional character's expression of kindheartedness came through again and again during the nine-year run of the series. John Walton Sr. remained true to his persona, his heart expression. Here was a guy you knew you could count on both within and outside his family. There are untold numbers of real-life people like John and families like the Waltons today who can be recognized for their kindheartedness.

The expressions of our character demonstrate our moral fiber. Jesus spoke of the heart's moral fiber when he said the expressions of some illustrate they are children of the devil (one who opposes) John 8:42-44.

We want to examine our personal expressions to see if our character reflectively resembles the character of God, which is demonstrated in the life of Jesus and defined in the following verses.

> *So that…you may become partakers of the divine nature…applying all diligence, in your faith supply moral excellence…knowledge…selfcontrol…perseverance…godliness…brotherly kindness…love. For if these qualities are yours and are increasing, they render you neither useless nor unfruitful in the true knowledge of our Lord Jesus Christ* (2 Peter 1:4-8).

Our heart's character traits speak of our dominant moral fiber—such as: honest or deceitful, kind or mean, loyal or shifty, charitable or selfish.

Attitude—Temperament

Attitude is the expression of our heart that demonstrates our temperament. The dictionary defines attitude as: "manner, disposition, feeling, position, etc., with regard to a person; tendency or orientation."

There are three categories of attitude: positive, negative, and neutral. People with positive attitudes notice the good rather than the bad and tend to be optimistic, cheerful, confident and flexible. People with negative attitudes notice the bad, complain about change, blame others for failure, and tend to be doubtful, jealous, angry, and frustrated. People with a neutral attitude don't pay much attention, ignore problems, and tend to feel discontented, indifferent, and apathetic.

Expressive Heart Reveals Us

Our attitude towards people, places, and things or situations determines the choices we make. While it is rare for someone to always be positive or negative, we generally bounce between different attitudes in different situations with a strong inclination toward one or the other. What type of temperaments might we express?

We can determine to have a positive attitude, as you will see in the following whimsical story:

There once was a woman who woke up one morning, looked in the mirror and noticed that she had only three hairs on her head. "Well," she said, "I think I'll braid my hair today." So she did and she had a wonderful day.

The next day she woke up, looked in the mirror and saw that she had only two hairs on her head. "Hmm," she said, "I think I'll part my hair down the middle today." So she did and she had a grand day.

The next day she woke up, looked in the mirror and noticed that she had only one hair on her head. "Well," she said, "Today I'm going to wear my hair in a ponytail." So she did and she had a fun, fun day.

The next day she woke up, looked in the mirror and noticed that there wasn't a single hair on her head. "Yea!" she exclaimed, "I don't have to fix my hair today!"

When we determine to enjoy each day with a positive and overcoming attitude like the woman in the story above, our life can be a joyful expression. No matter what we may go through, our attitude can be either sour or a sweet aroma.

> *But thanks be to God, who always leads us in triumph in Christ, and manifests through us the sweet aroma of the knowledge of Him in every place* (2 Corinthians 2:14).

Our attitude is not everything, but it does affect everything about us. The attitude we entertain affects how we think, feel, and understand (our conscious soul), and in turn, influences what we say and do.

What is our attitude about our circumstances? Do we say, "Good God, it's morning!" or "Good morning, God!" We want to examine our expressions to see if our attitudes reflect and resemble God's heart.

Our heart's attitude traits speak of our temperament—such as: loving or hateful, humble or proud, flexible or rigid, etc.

Attitude is our most important heart feature! *See Appendix IV: "Attitude Rules" on page 168.*

Personality—Social Behavior

Personality is the expression of our heart that demonstrates our social behavior. The dictionary defines personality as: "the visible aspect of one's persona as it impresses others: 'He has a pleasing personality'…"

A personality trait is the heart feature that illustrates social behavior. We all tend to express ourselves, mainly but not exclusively, as one of four personality types. Two types tend to be introverts: Melancholic (analytical, perfectionist) and Phlegmatic (amiable, peaceful); while two tend to be extroverts: Choleric (driver, powerful) and Sanguine (expressive, popular). Personality traits speak of our social behavior—such as: analytical, supportive, organized, or outgoing.

Let's look at a real life example of how personality affects our expression and life's work. In this story there are three siblings: two brothers and a sister. Each demonstrates one of the four general personality types.

The eldest brother is very outgoing—you'd say he's a people person. Some would call him a sanguine. He's definitely a leader and functions in a pastoral role. He's very comfortable speaking to groups of people.

The next oldest of the siblings is his sister. She's a somewhat shy person but is also very compassionate. She founded a home for orphans and has helped many kids to not only survive but learn to thrive. She isn't comfortable speaking to groups but her one-on-one skills are very effective. She has a melancholic personality.

The youngest of the three siblings is very laid back. He's rock steady and unflappable. When everything around him is up for grabs, he's calm and peaceful. Some see him as uncaring, but underneath, his mind is always working. He has a head for business and uses his prosperity to bless others wherever he sees a need. His personality type is phlegmatic.

All three of these siblings come from a solid godly home. They love the Lord with all their hearts, and yet they are all very different. Their personalities have led each of them down differing life paths.

Understanding our own personality type can help us recognize both our strong points and our weak ones. Whatever our personality type, we can learn to capitalize on our strengths and learn how to deal with our weaknesses so we can better reflect and resemble the heart of God and be a blessing to others.

Our heart's personality traits speak of our social behavior—such as: analytical, supportive, organized, or outgoing.

Renews and Develops

Every person is born with a heart that is ready to develop. We initially inherit our CAP qualities from our parents. The natural and spiritual environments we are raised in stimulate the development of our CAP. Our conscious assessment of our experiences and the choices we make strongly affect our heart's ongoing improvement or deterioration.

As the physical heart pumps either life-giving or tainted blood to our body, so our expressive heart emits either blessings or curses upon our self and on one another, to inspire or discourage. God wants to influence our heart so we are better able to bless and encourage one another.

> *Love the Lord your God with all your heart…with all your soul…with your mind…with all your strength* (Mark 12:30; Luke 10:27).

> *Let not your adornment be merely external…but let it be the hidden person of the heart, with the imperishable quality of a gentle and quiet spirit, which is precious in the sight of God* (1 Peter 3:3-4).

Some of us have not yet figured out who we are. Some simply excuse bad behavior and say, "That's just the way I am," as if their heart persona cannot change or improve. This however, is shortsighted.

Expressive Heart Reveals Us

We are all born into a world that is full of constant change. The earth thrives where it experiences changing seasons. What we tend to overlook is the fact that this life produces many changing situations to encourage us to adjust and change. We begin life as newborn babies, become adolescents, grow into adults, transform into parents, and eventually we mature into seniors. This life is all about change; we are all changeable. We can be better than we are now and do better than we have done in the past.

God created us to reflect and resemble Him as expressive beings. Don't forget, the Spirit of God already dwells in each of us as a life-giving part of what we are (body, soul, and spirit). We can all receive and learn from His expressions, especially from the expression of Jesus Christ.

We have observed in previous chapters that our soul's perceptions tend to develop into understandings—what we believe. Our belief, in turn, tends to rule our lives and provides direction to our overall activity. Consequently, what we believe has an influencing effect on our heart's expressions.

Whatever our soul believes about God, ourselves, and others affects the quality of our heart CAP. Our perceptions are observed by others in our expressions. Our heart attitude will reveal a strong self-centeredness just as it can illustrate a strong tendency toward godly values.

The biblical story of Mary and Martha illustrates how our beliefs have a profound effect on our heart and our overall behavior:

> *Now as they were traveling along, He entered a village; and a woman named Martha welcomed Him into her home. She had a sister called Mary, who was seated at the Lord's feet, listening to His word. But Martha was distracted with all her preparations; and she came up to Him and said, "Lord, do You not care that my sister has left me to do all the serving alone? Then tell her to help me." But the Lord answered and said to her, "Martha, Martha, you are worried and bothered about so many things; but only one thing is necessary, for Mary has chosen the good part, which shall not be taken away from her"* (Luke 10:38-42).

From this account, we can surmise these two sisters had differing views of how they should relate. Martha believed intense service and sacrifice were best. Mary believed attention to and understanding of the words of Jesus was paramount. These different beliefs had a profound effect on how they reacted to His presence. These two very different expressions were appreciated, while one was identified as the most beneficial.

Jesus encouraged us to learn of him so we can understand our heavenly Father's heart and become mature children:

> *Take My yoke upon you and learn from Me, for I am gentle and humble in heart, and you will find rest for your souls* (Matthew 11:29-30).

> *Draw near to God and He will draw near to you. Cleanse your hands…and purify your hearts* (James 4:8).

> *Therefore I urge you, brethren, by the mercies of God…do not be conformed to this world, but be transformed by the renewing of your mind, so that you may prove what the*

Expressive Heart Reveals Us

will of God is, that which is good and acceptable and [more] perfect (Romans 12:1-2).

Yes, we can change and become mature expressions of God's heart! Every one of us is able to receive life-changing insights and give ourselves to the renewing process of becoming a better person.

The Old Testament Hebrew word that is generally translated "new" in our Bible, *chadash*, also means "renew," "repair" and "rebuild."

> *Repent and turn away...cast away...your transgressions...make yourselves a new* [a renewed] *heart...repent and live* (Ezekiel 18:30-32).

> *I* [God] *will give you a new* [a renewed] *heart...I will remove the heart of stone...so you will be my people* (Ezekiel 36:26-27).

These quotes from Ezekiel may cause you to ask: Does God give us a new heart or do we make our hearts anew? Actually, it's a cooperative effort. As we repent (make efforts to turn from our error) and invite God into our life, He becomes our enabling source that helps us transform our soul's mind and our heart's attitude, so our actions can improve.

> *What does the LORD your God require from you, but to fear the LORD your God, to walk in all His ways and love Him, and to serve the LORD your God with all your heart and with all your soul...So circumcise your heart, and stiffen your neck no longer* (Deuteronomy 10:12, 16).

Isn't it interesting how the condition of our heart can be compared to a stiff neck (a posture of refusal)? When we stop refusing God's insightful help and submit in repentence, He will assist our heart's circumcision (cut unneeded excesses).

Heart of the Matter

Our Father demonstrated His loving heart in the life of Jesus Christ. Jesus illustrated God's love for us and invited us to receive Father's insightful guidance. God deeply desires us to receive expressions of His heart and learn to correctly imitate Him as His children:

> *Be imitators of God, as beloved children; and walk in love, just as Christ also loved you* (Ephesians 5:1-2).

> *Jesus said to him, "Have I been so long with you, and yet you have not come to know Me, Philip? He who has seen Me has seen the Father"* (John 14:9)

When we seek to imitate the example of Christ Jesus, our expressive heart is able to renew and begin to mature into suitable expressions of God's heart. Our mirroring of God's heart helps people to see and perceive God.

One mother in the movie, *War Room*, struggles with keeping her marriage together and her life on track. After coming to understand that God wanted her to give her problems to Him in prayer, she creates a prayer room out of her closet and sets out to pray for her marriage, which changes her own attitude and actions. Not long afterwards we see her daughter do the same and make her own list of things to pray for. At the end of the movie we see the wife, her husband, and her daughter all earnestly praying together. As a result of their prayers, they saw the importance of following God's ways, something that drastically changed their lives.

Expressive Heart Reveals Us

Work out your salvation…for it is God who is at work in you, both to will and to work for His good pleasure (Philippians 2:12-13).

Now the Lord is the Spirit, and where the Spirit of the Lord is, there is liberty. But we all, with unveiled face, beholding as in a mirror the glory of the Lord, are being transformed into the same image from glory to glory (2 Corinthians 3:17-18).

What is meant by the phrase "from glory to glory"? When God first draws us into an active fellowship and we accept Him into our heart's expressions, we experience an initial glory. When He puts His finger on our heart and begins to adjust our CAP, we experience another glory. When He shines His light on our relationships and we adjust our attitudes toward them, we experience yet another glory.

Some days we may slip back into old habits, but if we stay in His fellowship, we will continue to grow and mature. As we submit to our heavenly Father's "work in us" and "work out our salvation," our heart's CAP reforms, remolds, renews, and transforms who we are into better images and likenesses of God's heart. It's a process which begins and should continue throughout our lives. The apostle Paul wrote:

Brethren, I do not regard myself as having laid hold of it yet; but one thing I do: forgetting what lies behind and reaching forward to what lies ahead, I press on toward the goal…in Christ Jesus. Let us therefore…have this attitude… (Philippians 3:13-15).

God values our heart, who we are becoming as a person over

what we are as a being. While we are not sure exactly what we will be when we lose our natural body (1 Corinthians 15:44), we can be assured that God's purpose in our life does not cease:

> *Beloved, now we are children of God, and it has not appeared as yet what we will be. We know that when* [as] *He appears* [to us], *we will be* [become] *like Him, because we will see Him just as He is* (1 John 3:2).

Scripture confirms that it is our soul (what we think, feel, and believe) that is in need of salvation, to be saved from our conscious perceptions and commitment to erroneous ways of living. As we learn to think, feel, and believe (soul) in God's way of life, our heart expressions—who we are—will adjust and we become people who relate with godly values.

When we understand "what we are as a body, soul, and spirit being," it helps us focus on "who we are as expressive persons." We are all offspring of God, who through the tutoring fellowship of our heavenly Father, mature as children into better reflections of Him.

Memorize: *"For it is God who is at work in you, both to will and to work for His good pleasure"* (Philippians 2:13).

Questions to consider

1. What does God see when He looks beyond what we are?

2. How would you describe who you are?

3. What does God consider to be the most significant aspect of our life?

Chapter 5

Relational Concept Connects Us

A man was having a conversation with the Lord one day and said, "Lord, I would like to know what heaven is like."

The Lord then led him to two doors. He opened one of the doors and the man looked in. In the middle of the room was a large table. In the middle of the table was a large pot of stew, which smelled delicious and made the man's mouth water.

The people sitting around the table were thin and sickly. They appeared to be famished. They were holding spoons with very long handles that were strapped to their arms. Each found it possible to reach into the pot of stew and take a spoonful, but because the handle was longer than their arms, they could not get the spoons back into their mouths. The man shuddered at the sight of their misery and suffering.

The Lord said, "You have seen hell."

They went to the next room and opened the door. It was exactly the same as the first one. The large round table in the center held the same large pot of stew, which again made the man's mouth water. The people were equipped with the same long handled spoons, but here the people were plump and well nourished, laughing and talking as they ate.

The Lord said, "You have seen heaven."

The man said, "I don't understand."

"It is simple," said the Lord, "it requires but one skill. You see, these people have learned to feed each other, while the selfish ones in the first room only try to feed themselves."
—*Author unknown*

This story demonstrates the deeply rewarding value of our relational interactions. Our willingness to share with one another and recognize that others are as important as we are improves our life as well as theirs. The healthy way to live includes a care for one another.

A Relational God

We have seen in the first chapter, how the idea of mankind was first conceived in the mind of God as He desired to father offspring whom He could parent into His image and likeness. While God created the almost fathomless time and space universe with all its life forms, He relates to each of one of us as a parent. His declared intention to birth and grow offspring into mature children is recorded in Scripture:

> *Then God said, "Let Us make man* [mankind] *in Our image, according to Our likeness"* (Genesis 1:26).

Relational Concept Connects Us

While God reveals Himself to us in multiple ways, He relates to us primarily in three ways: God relates to us as a Father who oversees our birth and growth (Matthew 7:7-11); He relates to us as a Son to demonstrate His desire for us as His children (1 John 1:1-3); and God abides with us as a Spirit presence, to lead and guide us through our life processes (John 16:13). God is very relational!

God also created us as relational beings. What we have is a composition of body, soul, and spirit. Our soul consciousness is a blend of mind, will, and emotion. And our heart's character, attitude, and personality illustrate who we are as expressive persons.

Understanding what we are as a being and who we are as an expressive person allows us to begin to examine why God created us. The next chapters will focus more on why we exist.

We have examined how God declared His creative plan in the first chapter of Genesis, and then the second chapter describes how He made the first individual and remolded the one into two, making male and female. Together, they could be a better "one"—a relational completeness.

> *Then the Lord God said, "It is not good for the man* [individual] *to be alone; I will make him a helper suitable for him."...So the Lord God caused a deep sleep to fall upon the man...then He took one of his ribs and closed up the flesh at that place...fashioned into a woman...and brought her to the man* (Genesis 2:18, 21-22).

God declared one was "not good" because singularity, in His sight, is a sign of incompleteness. He created the one as a first step of a two-step process. Then He restructured the one into two. The first was simply a precursor to God's relational intention—completeness in relationship.

God utilized the relational first two to begin the ongoing process of making and forming His additional offspring through the human birth process.

> *The God who made the world and all things in it…made from one man every nation of mankind to live on all the face of the earth…for in Him we live and move and exist* (Acts 17:24-28).

The spirit of life in each of us came from God. Without His Spirit we are unable to live much less function. This is why the Apostle Paul said, "In Him we live and move and exist." This is true whether we realize it or not, even if we go so far as to deny it.

The first Adam was not perfect! *See Appendix V: "Mature Not Perfect" on page 174.*

Relational Reality

From humanity's beginnings, God established this relational concept as the primary process He would use to produce His offspring, who would develop under His care into various degrees of His image and likeness.

Some definitions can be helpful at this point. Relate means to have connection, meaningful interaction. Relationship: in touch with another, the condition or fact of being linked, joined, connected, associated, in harmony. Relationship terms: child, parent, spouse, offspring, friendship, fellowship, and community.

We are all birthed into life following the process of concep-

Relational Concept Connects Us

tion. After a number of developmental years, we can become a spouse and parent offspring of our own. Our children are extensions of us and the families we spring from. While some people are not able to birth children of their own, they still lend great value to the teaching and training of others. Our life includes many relationships, and God desires to be involved in each of them.

God's purpose in our life, beyond who and what we are, is realized in the relational interactions between us. We are incomplete and shortchanged when we are not in active fellowship with God and with each other.

During our human beginnings, a deceiver twisted God's stated purpose for us to insinuate we are supposed to be "as God," something more than offspring of God (Genesis 3:4-5; 2 Corinthians 11:3). Adam and Eve's acceptance of the scam planted in them an overly strong bent toward self-centeredness and an inflated view of "me, myself and I."

This complicated, in them, God's relational perspective. As a result, we all inherit an overly strong focus on our own importance. While everyone has contributing value and our self-awareness as a person is important, an inflated ego can be quite destructive to our self and to others.

Adam and Eve demonstrated what life is like both with God's relational perspective and without it. Before self-centered separation became their norm, they are described as being without shame, excuse, blame, or cover-up (Genesis 2:25). They only knew of God's relational concept.

When Adam and Eve accepted the "as God" perspective

from a deceiver, they immediately made clothes for themselves to cover their exposure from each other's view. Distrust began to develop between them and their ability to lovingly relate began to deteriorate.

Their ability to relate to God was also compromised. Their faith and trust in Father was obscured and confused by a resulting fear. When He came in the evening to visit, they were hiding. Instead of repenting, they made excuses and blamed another for their error (Genesis 3:1-13, 17).

They deviated from God's relational plan and their failure to repent (make an effort to change) began to hinder their growth into God's full intention. As our loving Father, God was bound to do something about it rather than leave them to continue in their error.

> *Then the LORD God said, "Behold, the man* [mankind] *has become like one of Us* [separated]…*and now, he might stretch out his hand, and take also from the tree of life, and eat, and live forever* [in separation]*"—therefore the LORD God sent him out from the garden of Eden…to guard the way to the tree of life* (Genesis 3:22-24).

While they were in their "as one" state of mind, God showed them loving mercy and removed their ability to eat of the Tree of Life, lest they live forever in their unrepentant state. As with Adam and Eve, in our separation from God we are still offspring; however, we are living in the limitations of our overly self-centered perspective. Thankfully we can repent of our separation and rebellious ways, enter into a receptive fellowship with God, and learn to be disciplined children.

Relational Concept Connects Us

But as many as received Him, to them He gave the right to become children of God (John 1:12).

This relational concept helps us get beyond the separating mentality of "me, myself and I." Our relational fellowships lend to transforming us beyond the limitations of an overly self-centered perspective.

A well-known speaker began his seminar by holding up a twenty-dollar bill. He asked everyone at the conference, "Who would like this new twenty-dollar bill?" Hands went up all over the room.

He said, "I'm going to give this twenty dollar bill to one of you, but first I need to crumple it." He wadded up the bill and asked, "Who still wants it?" Hands were quickly raised.

The speaker dropped the bill and ground it into the floor with his shoe. He picked up the crumpled, dirty bill. "Now who wants it?" Everyone still lifted their hands. "Friends, you have all learned a valuable lesson," the speaker concluded.

"No matter what I did to the money, you still want it because its value hasn't changed. Even though the bill is crumpled and dirty, it's still worth twenty dollars. Although someone may have been misused and abused, he or she still has infinite worth."

We want to see others and ourselves as valuable. Every person is precious in God's sight and should be in our sight as well. Every one of us is intended to learn and develop into mature children of God. When we relate to God and seek His insightful fellowship, our value actually improves because we partake of our "eternal source" of life.

Again, every person is important and each one of us can experience a better wholeness through active fellowships with our Father and with one another. God incorporated this relational purpose into our being so we could find a fulfilling completeness beyond self, in the interactive sharing of our life.

God's Image and Likeness

Let's look again at God's creative plan. We want to understand what He had in mind for us from the very beginning:

> *Then God said, "Let Us make man in Our image, according to Our likeness"…God created man in His own image and likeness…male and female He created* [initiated] *them* (Genesis 1:26-28).

This first mention of mankind identifies God's creative plan and intention for us. The second chapter of Genesis tells us something of the process He used to initially make the first two. The rest of Scripture details the ongoing process of birthing and making further offspring and children.

Most of us are familiar with the phrase from Genesis 1, "in the image and likeness of God." Many interpret this to mean that we are already in God's image and likeness. This view, however, overlooks the fact that the first couple was able to err, separate from God, and become less than what God proposed. God cannot be less than He is. They walked away from God and chose to live another way. So what we are "created to be" is still in need of being "formed and made."

When we look deeper into the scriptural account, we discover the Hebrew words translated image and likeness, can be translated as reflection and resemblance. Why is this important? It can help us understand God's intent. We are not made to be or act "as God," but to reflectively resemble Him as children.

Reflection speaks of the ability to mirror an image. The appearance of God in us is more of a reflective expression. Like a mirror, we reflect what is in our line of sight. The clarity of the godly impression we reflect is evidence of our close or distant fellowship with God.

> *But we all, with unveiled face, beholding as in a mirror the glory of the Lord, are being transformed into the same image from glory to glory* (2 Corinthians 3:18).

Resemblance speaks of a similar likeness. When a child imitates a parent, they show similar mannerisms that display like character, attitude, and personality (CAP). As offspring of God we are designed and intended, as good children, to resemble our Father's CAP. God's CAP is rooted in love. He cares for all His offspring, and our love for each other is to be an echo of His encompassing love.

> *Beloved, let us love one another, for love is from God; and everyone who loves is born of God and knows God. The one who does not love does not know God, for God is love…we also ought to love one another* (1 John 4:7-11).

We are not created as a being that is automatically the image and likeness of God. At best, we are created to be formed into the reflective resemblance of the heart CAP of God. My version of Genesis 1:26-28 would read like this:

> *Then God said, "We will make mankind to reflect and resemble My expressive heart"…So God created mankind to*

> be made into His own reflective resemblance…He initiated them, as male and female, to relationally become expressions of His heart."

As we observe God's heart and learn to reflectively resemble His CAP, we can become His intention and live as the delight of His heart.

Jesus said the primary relational concept that is to guide our life is an unrestricted love of God and an unqualified love for one another.

> *And one of them, a lawyer, asked Him [Jesus] a question, testing Him, "Teacher, which is the great commandment in the Law?" And He said to him, "You shall love the Lord your God with all your heart, and with all your soul, and with all your mind. This is the great and foremost commandment. The second is like it, you shall love your neighbor as your self. On these two commandments depend the whole Law and the Prophets"* (Matthew 22:35-40). Also see Mark 12:29-31; Galatians 5:13-14; Romans 13: 9-10.

The term "the Law and the Prophets" in that day spoke of "all Scripture." Jesus proclaimed, in essence, that relational love is the primary concept that underlies all that we have received as the written word of God. In other words, everything God has said to us is meant to teach us how to love our Father and respectfully love one another as family.

The Ten Commandments, which were given centuries before, are an expansion of this simplicity. Have you ever noticed how the first few focus on our relationship with God while

Relational Concept Connects Us

the rest focus on our relationship with one another? (See Exodus 20) The rest of Scripture expands on these Ten and the condensed two by describing what happens when we lovingly relate and what happens when we don't.

The Gospel of Luke records a lawyer asking, "What can I do to have eternal life?" Jesus responded with, "What does the Law say?" The lawyer replied, "Love God and your neighbor." Jesus complimented him with, "Correct, do this and you will live."

The lawyer then sought to justify selective love and asked, "Who is my neighbor?" Jesus replied with the story of a Good Samaritan (Luke 10:25-37). So Jesus turned the query, "Who should I love as a neighbor?" into the instruction, "Go and be a loving neighbor."

The point is: We should not qualify who is our neighbor as though they are or are not worthy of the status. Rather, we should be loving people who treat the people we encounter as neighbors no matter who they are. We qualify ourselves as a good neighbor by reaching out to meet the need of others.

The New Testament goes on to identify this relational concept as the Royal Law, which instructs us to be merciful and treat others the way we want to be treated. The term indicates that in God's eyes, we are royalty when we live by this standard.

> *However you want people to treat you, so treat them, for this is the Law and the Prophets* (Matthew 7:12).
>
> *As you want people to treat you, treat them in the same way...Be merciful, just as your Father is merciful* (Luke 6:31-36).

> *If…you are fulfilling the royal law… "You shall love the Lord your God and your neighbor as yourself," you are doing well* (James 2:8).

This relational concept enables us not only to properly relate to God as an exceptional Father but also helps us relate to one another as family. To the degree that we commit to God's relational approach to life, His perspective is restored in us and we are better able to partake of His presence among us. We want to accept and respect one another as family, with all our imperfections. Relating well with God and with one another is something we can all work on.

> Flatter me, and I may not believe you. Criticize me, and I may not like you. Ignore me, and I may not forgive you. Encourage me, and I will not forget you. Love me, and I may be forced to love you.
> —*William Arthur Ward*

Together Is Better

Have you ever wondered why most people have always had a tendency to gather in villages, towns, and cities?

> *They said, "Come, let us build for ourselves a city, and a tower whose top will reach into heaven, and let us make for ourselves a name, otherwise we will be scattered abroad over the face of the whole earth"* (Genesis 11:4).

In Genesis 11 it seems as though the reason was to keep them from being scattered and isolated throughout the whole earth. But there are other reasons: for protection, for access to other's talents and resources, for fellowship, and for social interaction. Even in their rebellious state, a desire to dwell together was still a motivating force in their lives.

Relational Concept Connects Us

> In the world today, 66% of countries have urban populations in excess of 50% of their total population. Worldwide 54% of the total population lives in urban settings. In the United States, 84% of the population lives in cities, and in the UK it's 91%. By 2030, it is projected that 66% of the world's population will be urbanized. —*United Nations News Center*

While we recognize our need for others and band together, many times we are unaware of God's relational purpose and fail to appropriately relate. So many people, so much busyness, but unfortunately so little intimate relationship!

A relational struggle is going on inside each of us. On the one hand, we have a godly desire to be joined to others, realizing we need them, want to receive from them, and want to contribute to their lives as well. On the other hand, there is a desire to be on our own saying, "I can do it myself; I'll prove it; leave me alone." This overly self-centered and self-sufficient tendency complicates most of our relationships.

The areas in our life that appear to be weak can become strengths when we reach out and encourage others to become a part of our lives and fill our areas of need. My areas of weakness—and we all have them—are no longer weak when I am joined to those who are able to complement my abilities with theirs.

> *Two are better than one because they have a good return for their labor. For if either of them falls, the one will lift up his companion. But woe to the one who falls when there is not another to lift him up...And if one can overpower him who is alone, two can resist him. A cord of three strands is not quickly torn apart* (Ecclesiastes 4:9-10, 12).

For example, when a crippled person and a blind person work together, they can say, "We are not handicapped." The one who cannot see can be guided by the one in the wheelchair. Likewise, the one in the chair can be pushed by the one who is blind. Together they can get somewhere faster and better than by themselves. Working together can create a synergy that brings multiplied benefits, as with a team.

Scripture says children of God who are in fellowship are "joint heirs" with Christ (Romans 8:17). Our active relationship with God and relational joining with others allow us to partake of God's presence (Christ-anointing) which comes to dwell with us, among us, and in our midst.

The spirit presence of God is felt by our spiritual senses more often than we know. We want to realize God is trying to get our attention. If we give His presence the time of day, we can receive insight, encouragement, and strength for each of our moments.

Some of us tend to acknowledge God's presence as Jesus, while others see Him as the Holy Spirit, or as our heavenly Father. It does not matter for they all refer to the same God.

> "You will know that I am in My Father, and you in Me, and I in you [relationally]"…Jesus answered…"If anyone loves Me, he will keep My word; and My Father will love him, and We will come to him and make Our abode with him" (John 14:17, 20, 23).

The relational approach to life is what we were designed for, but sometimes certain relationships can negatively affect us. Here is a warning exerted from Colin Powell's, *The Power of Association*.

> The less you associate with some people, the more your life will improve…As you grow, your associates will change. Some of your friends will not want you to go on. They will want you to stay where they are. Friends that don't help you climb will want you to crawl. Your friends will stretch your vision or choke your dream. Those that don't increase you will eventually decrease you. With some people you spend an evening: with others you invest in them. Wise is the person who fortifies his life with the right friendships. If you run with wolves, you will learn how to howl. But, if you associate with eagles, you will learn how to soar to great heights. —*Gen. Colin Powell (Ret.)*

Our personal relationships will affect how we see God and relate to Him. Some people will encourage us to seek God and His way of life, while others discourage us from doing so. If someone believes God does not exist, they will fight any acknowledgment or relational experience with Him. However, a believer, who is experiencing an active fellowship with God, will tend to encourage us to know God in the same way.

Relational Life

Everyone can observe God more clearly when we are relating well with others. My weakness in an area and your strength in that area, working together, illustrate a more complete picture of God's purpose in each of our lives. When we function together, onlookers are not sidetracked by areas of weakness but can observe and discern the wonders of God's presence with us, among us, and in our midst.

Today we see great diversity among believers. Some would call it divisions. The relational concept enables us to see diversity as healthy expressions of a multi-faceted God. Our differences, when we work together, are good for everyone.

Amos gave us a helpful insight that is often misunderstood and misused:

> *Can two walk together, unless they are agreed?* (Amos 3:3)

This scripture is often quoted to give credibility to division, as though it were saying: "I can't walk with you if we do not see eye to eye." The Word of God (in this mistaken reasoning) says, "The difference in our beliefs forbids our fellowship. We either agree or we part ways."

This verse is really saying: "We cannot walk together without agreeing to do so." We all walk a little differently, with different gaits and different speeds. Either we agree to fellowship together, sharing our differences during our walk, or we eventually won't be walking together.

Amos did not instruct us to walk only with people who think like us and separate from those who do not. In fact, Amos encouraged us to agree to walk together even though we are not alike in thought, actions, or preferences. We all benefit when we share what God is doing in our lives and consider what God is doing in others. Our personal experience is limited when we ignore the insightful experience of others.

Peter and Paul demonstrated this insight in the New Testament. Peter was recognized as the apostle to the circumcised and presented the Gospel to those who followed the

Law of Moses. Paul was recognized as the apostle to the nations and presented a slightly different Gospel to those who did not ascribe to the Law (Galatians 2:1-9). Yet they agreed to fellowship together and respect their differences.

We are all unique extensions of our Father and have a built-in need to relate to Him as the One who cares for us more than any earthly father. God created us as social beings that are intended to relate to each other as caring family members, even though we understand differently and live different lives. We just don't do very well when isolated from others.

God even relates to believers as functional groups, such as: sons of God, the body of Christ, the Church, a Temple, Israel, and the Kingdom. These terms do not address different groups but identify relational functions of the same people. Believers function as sons when responding to our Father, as the body of Christ when supporting one another, as a Temple when worshiping, as the Church when God is in our midst, as Israel and the kingdom of God when sharing God's insights with one another.

A proper understanding of this basic relational concept will help us abandon our habit of constantly pitting ourselves against each other. Instead of shying away from people who do not believe, worship, or live like us, we can reach out and share complementary values.

This is best accomplished when we properly relate to God as Father and to others as family. In this way, we hit the mark of God's intention for our life. Any real sense of wholeness, completeness, and fulfillment are only found in being part of functioning groups.

A relational, godly attitude allows us to partake of each other's experience and begin to see beyond the limitations of our own thoughts and experiences. We are all better off when we focus on what God is doing among "us," instead of seeing everything as though "I am central."

Intimate Relationships

Life is a series of relational experiences that allow us to have intimacy with others. Our intimate interaction with one another helps us grow into mature expressions of God's love. Intimacy enables us to experience enduring relationships, which bring stability to families and to society.

When you read and hear the phrase "intimacy with God," what comes to mind? Can you compare it to human intimacy? The writer of the Song of Solomon did. Intimacy on a personal level is evidence of a relationship that has gotten very deep, very personal, and very honest.

Many people are afraid of this kind of intimacy. They are afraid they may be exposed as ungodly, imperfect, or weak although we all have imperfections. They may also not want to pay the price and give of themselves. And yet we all need something more than a level of fellowship based on service; we desperately need intimacy.

God wants us to experience deeper levels of intimacy with Himself and with one another. When a man and a woman are joined in marriage, the Scripture says they become one flesh. The ultimate intimacy is to have levels of close sharing with people who are in active fellowship with God. The Apostle Paul put it this way:

Relational Concept Connects Us

Because of the surpassing greatness of the revelations…to keep me from exalting myself, there was given me a thorn in the flesh…Concerning this I implored the Lord three times that it might leave me. And He has said to me, "My grace is sufficient for you, for power is perfected in weakness." Most gladly, therefore, I will rather boast about my weaknesses, so that the power of Christ may dwell in me…Therefore I am well content…for Christ's sake; for when I am weak, then I am strong (2 Corinthians 12:7-10).

This kind of intimacy was lost in the Garden of Eden when our parents decided to partake of life without His guidance. As we have noted, when God came to commune with them in the cool of the day, as was normal at the time, they hid from His presence. Their decision to shun or disassociate with God brought separation into their relationship with Him and with each other.

Following Israel's deliverance from Egypt, God gathered them around Mt. Sinai to hear Him speak. Scripture tells us each person heard the voice of God, but they shrank from the one-on-one fellowship He offered. Not wanting to experience it again, they appointed Moses to mediate their communication with God (Deuteronomy 5:22-27; Exodus 20:1-19).

It was only after this event that God gave Moses the design for a tent to house His presence among them and the pattern for a priesthood to mediate His communication with them (Exodus chapters 23-31). Their lack of personal intimacy with Him is why that generation was unable to even believe what God told them through Moses.

Their previous perceptions of God kept that generation in a

servant mentality, unable to believe God could use them as victorious extensions of His ability to root out iniquity (Numbers 14:1-4). Instead of adjusting their hearts to become a people who would rule and reign with God, that generation died in their wilderness (Deuteronomy 1).

When Jesus ministered on earth, He prayed that all who believe in Him would become one in spirit with God and with each other (a relational oneness). That's the ultimate experience of relational fellowship!

> *I do not ask on behalf of these alone, but for those also who believe in Me through their word; that they may all be one; even as You, Father, are in Me and I in You, that they also may be in Us* (John 17:20-21).

Our relational interactions permeate every area of our lives: from our forming in the womb, growth in a family, joining in marriage, birthing and raising offspring, in our professions, and even in our demise. God designed life to be a series of relational experiences that help us grow and develop into expressions of God's love, which then flows among us.

> *Be imitators of God, as beloved children; and walk in love, just as Christ also loved you… Speaking the truth in love, we are to grow up in all aspects into Him who is the head, even Christ, from whom the whole body, being fitted and held together by what every joint supplies, according to the proper working of each individual part, causes the growth of the body for the building up of itself in love…*(Ephesians 5:1-5; 4:15-16).

Scripture reveals why we exist by identifying God's purpose

Relational Concept Connects Us

for creating us. We are birthed into this life as offspring of God, as imperfect beings, so we can mature into levels of completeness that is only found in relationships. We all need the maturing effects that come from our intimate interaction with God and with one another. Our differences are not intended to bring division. God intends our differences to lend diversity to our fellowships, which supplies insight to our understandings and strength to weaknesses.

The insightful contributions that come from our active fellowship with Father and with one another are what help mature us into better reflective resemblances of God's heart. We can have levels of intimacy with our heavenly Father. He equips us to better mirror Him in each of our life situations and circumstances.

Memorize: "*'You shall love the Lord your God with all your heart, and with all your soul, and with all your mind.' This is the great and foremost commandment. The second is like it, 'You shall love your neighbor as yourself.' On these two commandments depend the whole Law and the Prophets*" (Matthew 22:37-40).

Questions to consider

1. What is the primary concept Scripture wants to teach us?

2. What should become our primary life focus?

3. What is God's relational intention for your life?

Chapter 6

Father's Fellowship Nurtures Us

Me: "God, can I ask You a question?"
God: "Sure."
Me: "Promise You won't get mad?"
God: "I promise."
Me: "Why did You let so much stuff happen to me today?"
God: "What do you mean?"
Me: "Well, I woke up late…"
God: "Yes…"
Me: "My car took forever to start…"
God: "Okay…"
Me: "At lunch, they made my sandwich wrong and I had to wait…"
God: "Hmmm…"
Me: "On the way home, my phone went dead, just as I picked up a call…"

God: "All right…"

Me: "And on top of it all, when I got home I just wanted to soak my feet in my new foot massager and relax. But it wouldn't work! Nothing went right today! Why did You do that?"

God: "Let me see, the death angel was at your bed this morning and I had to send one of My angels to battle him for your life. I let you sleep through that."

Me: (humbled) "Oh…"

GOD: "I didn't let your car start because there was a drunk driver on your route that would have hit you if you were on the road."

Me: (ashamed but silent)

God: "The first person who made your sandwich today was sick, and I didn't want you to catch what they have. I knew you couldn't afford to miss work."

Me: (embarrassed) "Okay."

God: "Your phone went dead because the person that was calling was going to give false witness about what you said on that call. I didn't let you talk to them so you would be covered."

Me: (softly) "I see, God."

God: "Oh, and that foot massager, it had an electrical short that was going to knock out all of the power in your house tonight. I didn't think you would want to be in the dark."

Me: "I'm so sorry, God."

God: "Don't be sorry, just learn to trust Me.. in all things, the good and the bad."

Me: "I will trust You."

God: "And don't doubt that My plan for your day is always better than your plan."

Me: "I won't, God. And let me just tell you, God, thank You for everything today."

God: "You're welcome, child. It was just another day being your Father. I love looking after My children."

It is a wise father who knows his child. But it's a very wise child who takes time to know his father. —*Anonymous*

God is not only the Creator of the natural universe, He is your Creator. He is not only the Father of humanity, He is your Father. He is not only the Redeemer of mankind, He is your Redeemer! Doesn't it make a huge difference when you realize He is your personal Father?

Father's Heart

Humanity began in the mind of God before the progressions of time even started. As He desired to father offspring, He saw each one of us as children who would grow and develop under His parental care into reflective resemblances of His heart.

Unfortunately Adam and Eve chose to ignore God's guidance. The path they chose to follow was filled with the thick fog of self-centeredness that skewed their ability to see clearly and understand the Father's love. Our first parent's confusion led them to think of Him as an angry Father, and their fear created a separation in their relationship with God. They tried to hide from Him, as if anyone could (Genesis 3:8).

As a result of their choice, the differences between them began to appear as menacing contrasts instead of complements. Adam and Eve became suspect of each other, and their view of God and His love for them changed from unconditional (God's type of love) to conditional love. This guarded perception of love still hinders our relationships today.

In fact, after Genesis 2, the Old Testament does not even refer to God as Father. It appears that people from then on thought of God as a distant entity (Isaiah 59:2). Even today, we tend to think of God as One who is beyond our ability to know, communicate with, or understand.

The Old Testament record of God's dealings with mankind uses several names and compound titles, to speak of God. The primary names were:

Elohim means "ruler" and is translated God.

El Shaddai means "mighty one" and is translated Almighty.

Adonai means "master" and is translated Lord.

Yahweh means "Eternal One" and is translated Jehovah or LORD.

The Hebrews had no name or phrase to indicate God is our Father. Apparently the concept of God as Father vanished with the Garden of Eden until the advent of Jesus. When God's spoken word was incarnated as Jesus Christ, God reintroduced Himself afresh to humanity as our Father.

The Gospel of John is recognized as the most personal of the four Gospels. John's record of the life and ministry of Jesus relates more of the interaction Jesus had with God, noting Jesus speaking of God as Father 124 times. He even called the Temple in which they worshiped, His Father's house (John 2:16). Jesus continually spoke of God as Father and instructed everyone to begin to relate to Him as our Father:

> *Pray, then, in this way: "Our Father who is in heaven, hallowed be Your name"* (Matthew 6:9-10).

The New Testament speaks of God as Father more than 250 times! Yes, God is our Creator, King, and Judge, but He functions in these roles with the heart of a Father. As Creator, God oversees our growth. As King, He oversees the affairs of our world. As Judge, God administers corrective measures in our life.

The New Testament reveals God as our heavenly Father, who loves us as His own children. The new covenant also reveals how God sent His spoken word to us as a Son, as Jesus Christ, to demonstrate how we are to mature to reflect and resemble His heart.

Father-To-Child Attention

John's Gospel declared that when we accept the light that God sends into our world, we receive the right to be disciplined as Father's children:

> *There was the true Light which, coming into the world, enlightens every man...As many as received Him (the light of Christ), to them He gave the right to become children of God* (John 1:9, 12).

> *Blessed be the God and Father of our Lord Jesus Christ, who has blessed us...just as He chose us...before the foundation of the world...predestined us to adoption as sons...according to the kind intention of His will* (Ephesians 1:3-5).

Father's Fellowship Nurtures Us

These and other verses speak of our call into God's fellowship as an adoption. In the old Hebrew society, adoption took place when a son reached twelve years of age. Up until then, while fathers were involved at a distance, sons were raised primarily by their mother. A Bar Mitzvah acknowledged an offspring's adoption by his father. The father would then teach, train, and discipline the child in his ways. The child would learn how to act and function like the father so he could represent his father in the affairs of business (Luke 2:49). The following are additional verses regarding adoption into Father's discipline:

In love He predestined us to adoption as sons through Jesus Christ to Himself, according to the kind intention of His will (Ephesians 1:4-5).

God sent forth His Son, born of a woman...that we might receive the adoption as sons (Galatians 4:4-5).

All who are being led by the Spirit of God, these are sons of God. For...you have received a spirit of adoption as sons by which we cry out, "Abba! Father!" (Romans 8:14-15)

In adoption we become more than offspring who know God as a Provider, Lord, King, and Judge. We become children who learn to summit to Father's guidance, embrace His attitude regarding life, and are disciplined in His way of living.

Since the concept of fatherhood originated with the eternal God, we can count on Him being an ideal Father, better than the best earthly dad. As our Father, He promised us that through Christ, He would never leave or forsake us. His love will not allow Him to ignore or abandon us. Our Father's love is so far reaching that it is described as being limitless:

> *For I am convinced that neither death, nor life, nor angels, nor principalities, nor things present, nor things to come, nor powers, nor height, nor depth, nor any other created thing, will be able to separate us from the love of God* (Romans 8:38-39).

> A father: is respected because he gives his children leadership; is appreciated because he gives his children care; is valued because he gives his children time; and is loved because he gives his children the one thing they treasure most—himself.   —*Author unknown*

God not only wants our life to reflect Him, He offers an intimate Father-to-child fellowship with each of us, so we can draw from His expressive heart and learn of His character, attitude, and personality (CAP).

I can just see God smiling as each new baby is born—another life beginning a journey of adventure! What potential He sees in each of us! What love He has for us as He watches out for us along the way and offers the guidance we need to thrive!

His Guiding Presence

God is more than a Deity we worship and much more than a help during troubled times. God continually beckons us to draw from His perspective, learn of His ways, adapt His mannerisms, and be influenced by His caring attitude so we can be better expressions of His heart.

In order to become more reflective resemblances of our Father, we must be open to the fellowship of His guiding

Father's Fellowship Nurtures Us

presence. Fellowship is defined as a sharing of common interests, views, experiences, and goals. God understands where we are in our life process and wants to advise, lead, and guide us along the way through all our ups and downs.

We are more than pilgrims and strangers passing through this life. This life is more than an existence to be tolerated until we leave the natural realm. This life is where our existence starts and where we begin to grow into our created purpose as expressions of Father.

Our Father's care and concern for us is so strong that He continually calls, speaks, inspires, and offers direction to each of us, even to offspring who do not believe. Where do you suppose inspiring thoughts and new ideas come from? The spirit of life in each of us equips us to hear the inspiration God shares, especially if we are paying attention!

When God said, "I AM WHO I AM" (Exodus 3:14), He emphasized that He is the Ever-Present One. As the One who is always present, He is involved in everything between our start and our finish.

> *"I am the Alpha and the Omega," says the LORD God, "who is and who was and who is to come, the Almighty"* (Revelation 1:8).

As the Alpha and the Omega, God says He is the beginning and ending. He originated the universe and everything in it, including you and me. He will also be at every ending as our completer. This includes all of us.

Even the verse quoted above from the book of Revelation emphasizes the value of God's presence as the "I AM." Did you notice how He "who is" is noted before He "who was" and He "who is to come?" Since God is eternal, all past and future times are as the present to Him.

God wants us to know Him in our present situations and circumstances, more than from our past or in our future. Knowing who He was and who is yet to come does not compare with knowing Him as who is presently today. Our heavenly Father is available to each of us in our present times and situations; He is not far from any of us.

> *That they would seek God, if perhaps they might grope for Him and find Him, though He is not far from each one of us* (Acts 17:27).

We will have questions about good and evil as well as why many things seem to go wrong. Nevertheless, we can trust God will stay on our case, involved in our growth and development as our personal loving Father.

The peaceful benefits of partaking of God's guiding presence are available to each of us today. His presence in our present times offers an eternal quality to our life that is full of peace, joy, and righteousness.

> *For the kingdom of God is…righteousness and peace and joy in the Holy Spirit…So then we pursue the things which make for peace and the building up of one another* (Romans 14:17-19).

As our heavenly Father, God offers the guidance we need in our daily life and through the trials we encounter along the way. Remember, God's insightful presence can bring into our life His eternal values. God's eternal insights can help us deal with our passing times.

Father's Fellowship Nurtures Us

As offspring of God, we have His attention. Are we attentive to His abiding presence and responding to His loving care?

Child-To-Father Response

Every person is birthed into this life as an expression of God. We are all distinctively different because of two primary causes: First, our earthly parents pass on to us a new combination of slightly different DNA, which they inherited from their parents. Second, each of us, as offspring of God, receives only a measure of His spirit.

Because we are partial expressions of God, we need to be in active fellowship with Father, so we can absorb more of His perceptions and become better reflective resembles of His heart. Our human design enables us to sense and receive insight from Father, to learn of His ways.

> *This is eternal life, that they may know You, the only true God, and Jesus Christ whom You have sent* (John 17:3).

> *But let him who boasts boast of this, that he understands and knows Me, that I am the Lord who exercises lovingkindness, justice and righteousness on earth; for I delight in these things," declares the Lord* (Jeremiah 9:24).

Believers, who observe what the Father is saying and doing in our present times, tend to learn as children. The level of our response to His insightful presence enables us to be more intimate with Him.

Jesus told the story of a son who asked his father to let him spend his inheritance his own way, apart from his father's direction. The son then left home and spent the inheritance unwisely. He ended up scrounging for food in a pigpen. When he came to his senses, realizing his father's servants were much better off, he returned to his father's loving care. This is an allegory of the human race, of mankind's initial rejection and later acceptance of the love and guidance of our Father (see Luke 15:24).

While we live in the restrictions of this natural realm, our understanding of God remains somewhat limited. However, as we submit to our Father's guiding presence and experience His influencing reign in our life, we grow in our knowledge and understanding of Him.

The most effective way to learn about God is to approach Him as a child. Jesus demonstrated for us how a child/Father fellowship with God is designed to function.

> *I can do nothing on My own initiative…I do not seek My own will, but the will of Him who sent Me* (John 5:30).
>
> *Truly, I say to you, the Son can do nothing of Himself, unless it is something He sees the Father doing; for whatever the Father does, these things the Son also does in like manner* (John 5:19).
>
> *It is written in the prophets, "And they shall all be taught of God." Everyone who has heard and learned from the Father, comes to Me* (John 6:45).

We can now begin to understand how Jesus, as a human, knew what to do in the situations he encountered. Scripture says he was tempted just like us and could have erred (Hebrews 4:15). In this life, Jesus experienced the limitations of "children" of God, who do not know everything. It was the insight and inclinations he received from his ever-present Father that gave him the guidance needed in his moments.

As Jesus was about to leave this human experience and return to the glory he had with the Father as God's spoken word (John 17:5; 1:1-4), he instructed his followers to communicate with God as a caring Father:

> *Truly, truly, I say to you, if you ask the Father for anything in My name, He will give it to you…for the Father Himself loves you* (John 16:23, 27).

Could Jesus have been any clearer? Our response to God is ideally demonstrated as child-to-Father. As offspring, with a measure of His Spirit, we can all experience His presence and receive His insightful guidance. However, when we approach Him as a child seeking the Father's guidance, we are more receptive to the insight He desires to give.

> *Jesus said to him, "I am the way, and the truth, and the life; no one comes to the Father but through Me"* (John 14:6).

What did Jesus mean by this statement? We have found this verse can be translated a little differently, as:

> *Jesus said to him, "I am the truthful way to live. No one knows God as Father without being an obedient son"* (John 14:6, my version).

I have shown this translation to Greek linguists. They confirm my translation of this verse could be appropriate. It is also supported by the other passages we have cited and many others as well.

God does not want us to see Him as a boss whose favor depends on our performance. Nor does He want us to think of Him so much as our King or Judge. Above all, we want to see God as our loving Father.

> *See how great a love the Father has bestowed on us, that we would be called children of God; and such we are…Beloved, now we are children of God* (1 John 3:1-2).

A Mentor

Because we are so slow at learning to hear and follow the revealing insights God provides, He also gives us mentors—those who can come alongside as an insightful father, to help us through the difficulties we face.

For example, Paul mentored Timothy and called him "my true child in the faith" (1 Timothy 1:2). He also worked closely with the church as seen in the following verses he wrote to the Corinthian assemblies:

> *I do not write these things to shame you, but to admonish you as my beloved children. For if you were to have countless tutors in Christ, yet you would not have many fathers, for in Christ Jesus I became your father through the gospel. Therefore I exhort you, be imitators of me* (1 Corinthians 4:14-16).

A note here on Paul's intent in the statement "Be imitators of me" can be important. Godly mentors lead, counsel, and encourage us to hear God and follow Him, not the mentor. This is clarified in Paul's other writings:

> *Brethren, join in following my example, and observe those who walk according to the pattern you have in us* (Philippians 3:17).

Father's Fellowship Nurtures Us

> *Remember those who led you, who spoke the word of God to you; and considering the result of their conduct, imitate their faith* (Hebrews 13:7).

> *Therefore be imitators of God, as beloved children; and walk in love, just as Christ also loved you and gave Himself up for us* (Ephesians 5:1-2).

In His wonderful concern for us as our Father, God sends us people who can share from their insightful experience. These mentors are not to take the place of God's revealing presence in our life, but they support our childlike response to God as the real guiding force in our life. We want to be as children and respond to His input, whether through mentors or directly in our child-to-Father fellowship with God.

When we spend time reading Scripture, listening to the still small voice of God, and entertaining His ever-abiding presence among us, we get to know our heavenly Father and become better expressions of His heart. As our fellowship with God deepens, so does our desire to please Him and draw others into the wonderful life He wants us to live.

> *Godliness is profitable for all things, since it holds promise for the present life and also for the life to come. It is a trustworthy statement deserving full acceptance…* (1 Timothy 4:8-10).

As we respond to His guidance and learn of His CAP, we are better able to reflect God's heart in whatever we do, whether it's as a farmer, carpenter, computer tech, teacher, parent, or teen-ager. Our designed purpose involves who we are as a person and includes all of our "what" components, as well as what we say and do.

No matter how much we try to run away from this thirst for the answer to life, for the meaning of life, the intensity only gets stronger and stronger. We cannot escape these spiritual hungers. —Ravi Zacharias

Everyone can become! *See Appendix VI: "Called and Chosen" on page 178.*

Insightful Fellowship

God has always desired to dwell in the midst of His children as He had once done in the Garden with Adam and Eve.

I will dwell among…and will be their God (Exodus 29:45).

For we are the temple of the living God; just as God said, "I will dwell in them (in their midst) and walk among them" (2 Corinthians 6:16).

God wants to be our ever-present guide through life. When He sent Jesus to dwell among us and illustrate Father's desire to dwell with us as a presence, it was declared:

…and they shall call His name Emmanuel, which translated means, "God with us" (Matthew 1:23).

The resurrected Jesus also declared that he would be "in our midst" (as God's presence) when two or more are gathered in his name.

For where two or three have gathered together in My name, I am there in their midst (Matthew 18:20).

When we interact in godly ways and share what God is saying and doing, we invite His presence to become more ob-

Father's Fellowship Nurtures Us

vious. Our interactive fellowship with God in our midst transforms us into reflective resemblances of His heart (2 Corinthians 3:18; Ephesians 1:9-11). Our pursuit of the Father and His way of life (as described in my book, *The Christ Culture*) helps establish us in our destiny.

Our growth as children into reflective resemblances of God's heart takes place in the midst of our fellowship with Him and one another. What is fellowship? You often hear the phrase, "We had some great fellowship last night!" Scriptural fellowship is much more than a good time together.

> *But if we walk in the Light as He Himself is in the Light, we have fellowship with one another, and the blood of Jesus His Son cleanses us from all sin* (1 John 1:7).

Scripture says real fellowship with God flows from walking in the light and living the kind of life that we would not be embarrassed for others to see. When our lives are open and transparent before the Lord and one another (as in "being real" and not fake), we are willing to admit our faults to God and one another. God calls us to a much deeper level of fellowship with Him and with each other. He nurtures us in those relationships.

Prayer

The Father's nurturing also takes place during our times of personal prayer and meditation. Prayer connects us not only to God's provisions but more importantly to a place of fellowship in His presence.

When the disciples asked Jesus how to pray, he gave these instructions:

> *When you pray, go into your inner room, close your door and pray to your Father who is in secret* (Matthew 6:6).
>
> *Pray, then, in this way: "Our Father who is in heaven, hallowed be Your name. Your kingdom come. Your will be done, on earth as it is in heaven. Give us this day our daily bread. And forgive us our debts, as we also have forgiven our debtors. And do not lead us into temptation, but deliver us from evil. For Yours is the kingdom and the power and the glory forever"* (Matthew 6:9-13).

Many people suppose that prayer is a way to appeal to God for forgiveness, provision, and protection. While these are valid prayerful goals, the prayer Jesus instructs us to pray presents us with three primary objectives: To acknowledge God as Father, to honor His name (identity), and to welcome His kingdom (ruling) influence into our lives.

Jesus' emphasis in prayer is toward acknowledging and building our relationship with Father. I guess a question we should ask ourselves from time to time is: Are we seeking the hand of God or the face of God?

Biblical prayer is our two-way conversation with God. When Scripture says we are to pray without ceasing (1 Thessalonians 5:16-18), it speaks of living in an attitude of prayer. A prayerful attitude postures us to be open to our interaction with Father throughout the day.

When we make our requests known (Philippians 4:6), we want to listen for God's response. God doesn't always grant what we ask. He may want us to realize He will not answer as we desire, or maybe the answer will come at a later time, or

Father's Fellowship Nurtures Us

perhaps our desire does not agree with His will in the matter. He may even have something better in mind.

This is the confidence which we have before Him, that, if we ask anything according to His will, He hears us (1 John 5:14).

This verse says God hears us. It does not say that He will fulfill all our requests. Our Father is not a vending machine in which we put in the right prayer and out pops what we ordered. No, He is a loving Father who puts our welfare above our desires. We should be asking for His guidance as we deal with things, then listening for His still small voice to provide the insight we need for the situation.

Someone once said that God always knows how to get His word through to us, regardless of our spiritual sensitivity. If we are dull of hearing, God has dynamite. If we are sensitive, he has a gentle breeze. In the Old Testament one of God's prophets, Balaam, was displeasing to the Lord. On his way to a particular event, God got his attention by speaking through the mouth of his donkey (Numbers 22:21-23). Either way, God is most always trying to communicate with us. God invites us to partake of His fellowship as our Father and be taught as children who see, hear, and are led by His guiding presence (John 17:18; 20:21). Isaiah encouraged us to:

Come and let us go up…that He may teach us concerning His ways, and that we may walk in His paths (Isaiah 2:3).

May God, by the presence of His Holy Spirit, restore a true expression of family to our lives! God wants to share His eternal life with us today, as a Father, and He wants us to share the quality of life He gives us with others in His family. Our sharing begins in our homes, toward our children, siblings, and parents. Are we helping or hindering this purpose?

Memorize:

> *See how great a love the Father has bestowed on us, that we would be called children of God; and such we are. For this reason the world does not know us, because it did not know Him* (1 John 3:1).

Questions to consider:

1. What is the real value in knowing God as Father?

2. Which view of God is most helpful for us: Creator, the Deity, the Almighty, Lord, King, Judge, or parental Father? Why?

3. How do we realistically partake of the kingdom of God today?

Chapter 7

Will of God Directs Us

A professor stood before his philosophy class and had some items in front of him. When the class began, he wordlessly picked up a very large, empty mayonnaise jar and proceeded to fill it with golf balls. He then asked the students if the jar was full. They agreed that it was.

The professor then picked up a box of pebbles and poured them into the jar. He shook the jar lightly. The pebbles rolled into the open areas between the golf balls. He then asked the students again if the jar was full. They agreed it was.

The professor next picked up a box of sand and poured it into the jar. Of course, the sand filled up everything else. He asked once more if the jar was full. The students responded with a unanimous, "Yes."

The professor then produced two Cokes from under the table and poured the entire contents of both into the jar effectively filling the empty space between the sand. The students laughed. "Now," said the professor as the laughter subsided, "I want you to recognize that this jar represents your life.

"The golf balls are the important things—your family, your children, your health, your friends, and your favorite passions—and if everything else was lost and only they remained, your life would still be full. The pebbles are the other things that matter like your job, your house, and your car. The sand is everything else—the small stuff.

"If you put the sand into the jar first," he continued, "there is no room for the pebbles or the golf balls. The same goes for life. If you spend all your time and energy on the small stuff, you will never have room for the things that are important to you. Pay attention to the things that are critical to your happiness. Spend time with your children. Spend time with your parents. Visit with grandparents. Take your spouse out to dinner. Take care of the golf balls first—the big things that really matter.

"Set your priorities. The rest is just sand. One of the students raised her hand and inquired what the Cokes represented. The professor smiled and said, "I'm glad you asked. The Cokes just show you that no matter how full your life may seem, there's always room for a couple of Cokes with a friend."

And those times with friends—our fellowship with others—are the things that fill out our life and complete it like nothing else can. They give us the place wherein we can share with one another the godly qualities and choices we are learning from Him.

"The Lord never hides His will from us. In time, as you obey the call first to follow, your destiny will unfold before you. The difficulty will lie in keeping other concerns from diverting your attention." —*Charles R. Swindoll*

Spoken and Revealed

When God fused His Spirit into the first human body, spirit became the life-giving component in what Adam was as a human being (body, soul, and spirit). As offspring of the first couple, we all receive and partake of similar physical bodies and the same life-giving spirit.

Because we all have a spirit that connects us to the heavenly realm, each of us can hear the promptings of God's Spirit and come to understand His will for us. When we include a relational fellowship with God as one of our most important priorities, we are able to experience His reigning influence in our lives and in essence, partake of the kingdom of God.

Two thousand years ago, God sent His spoken expression into the earth to live, die, and resurrect as Jesus Christ.

> *In the beginning was the Word* [Greek logos – spoken expression], *and the Word was with God, and the Word was God…All things came into being through Him* [God's logos – spoken expression]…*The Word became flesh, and dwelt among us…No man has seen God…the only begotten…has explained Him* (John 1:1-3,14, 18).
>
> *And He is the image* [expressed resemblance] *of the invisible God and the firstborn* [preeminent] *of all creation.* (Colossians 1:15).

God's heart expression (His spoken word) lived on the earth as Jesus Christ. He was a clear example of God's will for children who are learning to relate and become mature reflective resemblances of Father:

> *For I have come down from heaven, not to do My own will, but the will of Him who sent Me* (John 6:38).

God's will for us can be observed in the life example that is provided in the "incarnate word" of Jesus Christ (John 1:1-4; 1 John 1:1-3). We can also read about God's will for us in the "written word" of Scripture (John 5:39). We can even hear the will of God for us expressed in the "spoken word" of God's abiding presence (1 Kings 19:12; John 14:16).

These expressions of God reveal His will for everyone in general and for each one of us individually. His will is revealed to us as we partake of the insights His eternal Spirit reveals. We then experience His will by yielding our will to His revealing expressions (written, displayed, and spoken).

Our birth into life means we all receive the spirit of life (Acts 17:26). This spirit comes from our heavenly Father and eventually returns to Him (Ecclesiastics 12:7). So, every living human being, good and not so good, is an offspring of God; no one is void of His life-giving Spirit.

Our spirit gives each of us an inherent ability to hear and receive from God, a call to unite with Him in fellowship, and the potential to mature into His reflective resemblance. Our ability, calling, and potential, however, are invitations not guarantees. This is how John put it:

Will of God Directs Us

The true Light which, coming into the world, enlightens every man...As many as received Him [the Light of God in Christ], *to them He gave the right to become children of God* [tutored offspring], *even to those who believe...who were born...of the will...of God* (John 1:9-13).

We are all birthed into life as offspring of God who need to experience the Father's guidance so we can become disciplined and trained children and be better expressions of His will.

Shown and Demonstrated

The experience of one of the early followers of Christ, Paul the apostle, illustrates several ways the will of God is expressed and known. Before Paul's conversion, he was known as Saul, a religious man who excelled among his colleagues and persecuted followers of Christ (Acts 8:1-3).

One day he was travelling down the road when a blinding light shone from above. Saul fell from his mount and a voice from heaven spoke, "Saul, Saul, why are you persecuting Me?" He was then instructed to go into the city where he would be told what to do (Acts 9:1-6).

After being blinded by the light, he was led into Damascus where he prayerfully waited. Then the Lord sent a man named Ananias to pray for him to receive his sight and be immersed in the presence of God's Spirit (Acts 9:7-19).

Paul spent the next three years communing with God and receiving insight (Galatians 1:13-19). This was a time when his understanding of God's will was revised from the Jewish perspective in which he was schooled. It was such a fresh view of

God's will that church leaders who had spent three years with Jesus said they found it hard to understand (2 Peter 3:16).

Let's fast forward a few years to Paul's second visit to Jerusalem and notice how the apostles and elders, under the guidance of God's presence, adjusted their perception of the necessities of the faith:

> *It seemed good to the apostles and the elders, with the whole church, to choose men from among them to send to Antioch with Paul and Barnabas…it seemed good to the Holy Spirit and to us to lay upon you no greater burden than these essentials* (Acts 15:22, 28).

God used dreams and visions to speak and reveal His will. To prepare for an exchange between a godly man who did not know Christ and the Apostle Peter, visions were given. In one vision, God instructed the Roman centurion Cornelius, to seek out Peter for clarifying instruction. He also spoke to Peter in a vision so he would be willing to spend time with the Gentile, a difficult thing for a Jew of that day (Acts 10:1-23).

During the process of Jesus' birth, God spoke to Joseph three times in a dream; once to announce Mary's pregnancy, once to warn of Herod's effort to kill the child, and once to say it was safe to return home. God also spoke to the Wise Men in dreams (Matthew 1:20; 2:12-22).

Forty days after the resurrection of Jesus, on the day of Pentecost, God showered His Spirit presence upon followers who were waiting for his empowering return. Peter recited to the gathering crowd a prophesy God gave centuries earlier about the event they were now experiencing.

Will of God Directs Us

But this is what was spoken of through the prophet Joel: "And it shall be in the last days," God says, "that I will pour forth of my Spirit on all mankind; and your sons and daughters shall prophesy, and your young men shall see visions, and your old men shall dream dreams...both men and woman" (Acts 2:16-18).

Let's review some of the ways God shares His will with us, beyond the written Scriptures: 1) an audible voice spoke to Paul; 2) a reorientation of Paul's understanding during three years in the desert; 3) a consensus of opinion among believers; 4) a vision to Peter and to an unbeliever; and 5) by dreams to Joseph and the Wise Men.

So the question we ask now is: does God actually speak to us in our everyday lives? A friend of mine used to carpool with a buddy to their places of employment. They worked in two different locations a few miles apart. One afternoon, my friend pulled into the parking lot where his carpool buddy worked. After a few minutes someone came out to tell my friend to go on without the rider. So he did, but after driving a few minutes he felt very strongly that he should go back and look for the rider. He turned the car around and went back (this was well before cell phones).

As he waited in the parking lot again, he wondered if he had heard from God. There was no audible voice, not even a "still small voice," just a nagging feeling he needed to return. After a few minutes, his rider came out of the building, surprised to see my friend. He explained that his boss was going to give him a ride home but the ride had fallen through. The man would have been stuck 20 miles from home if my friend had not heard from God.

God can speak to us in a variety of ways. It can be as a gentle nudge or inclination, through an off the wall comment someone makes, in an inspirational new thought, or in an instruction from a parent or mentor. God is only restricted by our lack of attention or willingness to hear.

Each of us can receive fresh and inspiring thoughts as God shares elements of His will for us as an individual. God wants to lead and guide each of us into a better life experience.

God's sharing presence can also produce a cleansing and refreshing effect, like running water (Ephesians 5:26). It can produce fruitfulness in our life (Luke 8:11-15; James 1:21-25). Why would we ever not want to listen to Him?

How wonderful that God not only teaches us through His written word but also directs us through a personal word as we need it! God's spoken word conveys and reveals to us His will, both in general and specific ways.

Abiding Presence

God has always sought to dwell among us as an enlightening and empowering presence. Following Adam's error, God offered direction to Adam's son (Cain) and it was rejected. When God's abiding presence was offered to Israel, they rejected it and restricted His communication with them (Exodus 20:19).

> *For I am convinced that neither death, nor life, nor angels, nor principalities, nor things present, nor things to come, nor powers, nor height, nor depth, nor any other created thing, will be able to separate us from the love of God* (Romans 8:38-39).

Paul said nothing (no external force or thing) can separate us from God's love. However, our own efforts can keep us from receiving the love He offers. Israel's history in the Promised Land as a people shows every third generation turned a deaf ear to God's guidance (Judges 2:10 – 4:1).

A caution at this juncture can be important. History shows us that when we hear and see what God says and does, we can settle for that word or experience and hinder our ability to receive additional insight. The people of Israel settled for the Law of Moses, when God intended for the Law to lead them to Christ, to help them accept the experience of God among them and in their midst (Exodus 25:8; Galatians 3:24).

As Israel of old, too often we settle for what God has said in our past and build safeguards that make it difficult to see or hear fresh insight. We take the words we have received about God and the life He wants us to live, solidify them, add a few extraneous ideas as supports, and then we become experts. We stand strong on our revelation and even complicate the ability of those around us to consider greater light.

While there are many examples, a few major ones in recent history will illustrate our point. The Reformation of the 1500s revealed that faith and salvation is more than a religious system. It was not until the Great Awakening revivals of the 1700s that believers began to realize we could experience a forgiving cleanse through God's presence. Then it wasn't until the early 1900s that believers began to realize we can experience immersions in His Spirit presence. Each visitation brought new light to live by. People, however, settled into their visitation and began to build walls to protect what was revealed, which limited their ability to hear and receive more.

Children are intended to grow and develop. Our growing development as children of God requires us to stay soft throughout our life, so we can continue to absorb what God is saying and doing today. Growing children are also intended to cease with our childish or elementary ways (1 Corinthians 13:11).

Don't forget, when God instructed Abraham to sacrifice his son Isaac, He did not intend for Abraham to slay his son, it was an exercise in obedience. If Abraham had been unable to receive a fresh and different word from God, he would have killed Isaac. Are we settling for what God has said in the past and missing His developing intent? Abraham's softness before God allowed him to be called the father of all believers (Galatians 3:6-7).

Illustrated Love

The following story shows how one woman's softness to God and trust in Him gave her the courage to save her children from certain death, no matter the consequences to herself. She was indeed a reflective resemblance of God's love for her children.

It had started as a wonderful day. Joy Veron was on a vacation with her family in the mountains of Colorado. The trip had been idyllic, and they were preparing for one last swim before driving home to Texas.

Then disaster struck. Her three small children, aged between two and seven, ran ahead and got into the family SUV. Its engine was running and it was parked next to a cliff, which led down to a deep canyon. In seconds, the car slipped into

Will of God Directs Us

gear and started to roll. Instinctively, Joy threw herself underneath the wheels of the SUV to stop it from rolling over the cliff with her children inside.

"I remember feeling it begin to run over me. I fell backwards, and the front of the car caught me by the heels. I did like a somersault under the car and the third time it hit, I knew that it broke my back. I was 30 years old and the life I knew was gone."

But she had done enough. Her sacrifice had slowed the car's momentum just enough to allow her father to rush over and hit the brakes. Her children were safe. However, Joy was so severely injured that everybody thought she was going to die. Her children stood around her crying as the paramedics were called.

Joy remembers, "It was like this voice said, 'You've got a choice here...You can go on if you want to tell your kids goodbye and say those parting words, but if you want to [stay], you've got to fight.' And when I heard them screaming, I knew I had to fight."

Her children, Chloe, Annie, and Elliot, are thriving today: Chloe has just graduated from Harvard, and Elliot says that his mother is his inspiration. But Joy herself, now 46, never walked again. Although Joy may never walk, her reward is great in seeing her children thrive. What a difference a choice can make!

—Adapted from: http://www.dailymail.co.uk

Our Father desires to lead, guide, teach, train, and discipline each of us so we can better relate to Him and to one another:

The Spirit Himself testifies with our spirit that we are

children of God...heirs of God and fellow heirs with Christ (Romans 8:16-17).

Heirs of God are those who are responsive to Father and are discipled into His character, attitude, and personality. They learn to be reflective resemblances of God in ways similar to Christ Jesus, as joint heirs, who demonstrate God's sacrificial love. When we respond to Father's loving guidance, as Jesus did, we learn to be children indeed and develop into more mature expressions of God. He wants all of His "offspring" to become responsive "children" who receive His instructions. What an awesome privilege!

Let us not be restricted by the insightful revelations of our past or by our prideful protection of what we have known. God's will for us is to ascend into greater heights as children of our Almighty Father. We can be better reflective resemblances of our Father, illustrations of His light!

Our Father is our light! *See Appendix VII: "Light of Life" on page 182.*

Spirit Perspective

Life speaks of activity, while death denotes a lack of activity. Scripture tells us that if we are not experiencing an active fellowship with God, our spirit is "as dead" to Him (Ephesians 2:1-5; 5:8-10, 14). Jesus even spoke of spiritually inactive people as the living dead (Matthew 8:22).

The life of God, which we are to draw from, is much more than physical life. It is a shame, but the New Testament translators rendered many Greek words into the English word "life" and hid a good bit of meaning.

There are three Greek words translated as "life" that specifically refer to either the body, soul, or spirit component in us. These three very different words address different aspects of our life experience. Let's look at each:

One Greek word that is translated "life" is *bios*, which speaks of the physical (biological) activity of our natural body (it occurs 10 times).

Another Greek word translated "life" is *psuch*, which speaks of the mind, will, and emotional activity of our conscious soul (it occurs 101 times).

The third Greek word that is translated simply as "life" is *zoe*, which speaks of our spirit's activity, the life of our spirit (it occurs 135 times).

Scripture's abundant use of zoe amplifies the importance of our spirit life. Our bios (physical) eye can only see what is natural, which is temporal and passing away. However, our zoe (spirit) eye can observe spirit realities such as one another's character, attitude, and personality.

As the true light that enlightens the world comes from God, so our life sustaining, spiritual nourishment comes from God. Our interaction with God is compared to eating the bread of life. If we draw insight from the life of Jesus, it produces a lifelong satisfaction to our hunger and thirst for life:

> *Jesus then said to them, "Truly, truly, I say to you…it is My Father who gives you the true bread out of heaven. For the bread of God is that which comes down out of heaven, and gives life [zoe] to the world." Then they said to Him, "Lord, always give us this bread." Jesus*

> *said to them, "I am the bread of life* [zoe]; *he who comes to Me will not hunger, and he who believes in Me will never thirst"* (John 6:32-35).

If we are continually partaking of this bread of life, our spiritual hunger and thirst tend to continually find satisfaction. May we partake daily of this source of spirit life. When God sent His spoken expression into the earth as Jesus Christ, He went to lengths to demonstrate to us His desire to be an intimate part of our life. God wants to dwell as a presence in our midst, as a zoe life. Here are a few of the many verses that speak specifically of a spirit led life.

> *"I* [Jesus] *came that they might have* [zoe: spirit] *life, and might have it more abundantly"* (John 10:10).

> *"This is the will of My Father, that everyone who beholds the Son and believes in Him, may have eternal* [zoe: spirit] *life"* (John 6:40).

> *The free gift of God is eternal* [zoe: spirit] *life in Christ* (Romans 6:23).

> *Jesus said…"I am the way, the truth, and the* [zoe: spirit] *life"* (John 14:6).

Too often these verses are relegated to an afterlife. While this futuristic view is true, it also applies to our lives today. When Jesus said; "I am the truthful way to spiritually live" (my version of John 14:6), He referenced His Son-to-Father fellowship with God. Jesus showed us how to actively fellowship with our Father and live a spiritual life (John 5:19; 12:50). Our fellowship with God permits His insight to improve our views so we can understand more as eternally minded people.

The abundance of spirit life is not just an existence for an afterlife, it is for us today.

Remember, our soul consciousness can comprehend the realities of both the natural and spiritual realms. The senses of our spirit enable us to partake of spiritual realities, to receive the eternal insights God reveals, and to lend support to each other's spiritual livelihood.

Paul said the exercise of our spirit senses aide our maturity:

> *For everyone who partakes only of milk is not accustomed to the word of righteousness, for he is an infant. But solid food is for the mature, who because of practice have their senses trained to discern good and evil* (Hebrews 5:13-14).

When we fellowship with God and act on what He says, we experience our Eternal Father and learn to live a Spirit-led life. Scripture calls this fellowship of our spirit with God's Spirit—eternal life (John 17:3). We can experience the spiritual dimension right here and now, in various degrees.

Our spirit perspective—how we see and respond to our heavenly Father and to one another—is very important. Scripture shares much insight about God's will for our natural and spiritual life in the following verses:

> *He has told you, O man, what is good; and what does the LORD require of you but to do justice, to love kindness, and to walk humbly with your God?* (Micah 6:8)

> *And He said to him, "You shall love the LORD your God with all your heart, and with all your soul, and with all your mind." This is the great and foremost commandment. The second is like it, "You shall love your neighbor as*

> *yourself. On these two commandments depend the whole Law and the Prophets"* (Matthew 22:37-40).
>
> *Live in peace with one another…always seek after that which is good for one another and for all people. Rejoice always; pray without ceasing; in everything give thanks; for this is God's will for you in Christ Jesus* (1 Thessalonians 5:13-18).
>
> *Finally, brethren, rejoice, be made complete, be comforted, be like-minded, live in peace; and the God of love and peace will be with you* (2 Corinthians 13:11).

We are created to be relational people, who relate to our heavenly Father and relate to one another. May we be godly contributors in all our relationships!

Our Choice

During our human beginnings in the Garden of Eden, God gave Adam and Eve a vast amount of freedom with only one basic restriction.

> *And the LORD God commanded…"From any tree of the garden you may eat freely; but from the tree of the knowledge of good and evil you shall not eat, for in the day that you eat from it you shall surely die"…And the serpent said…"You surely shall not die! For God knows that in the day you eat from it your eyes will be opened, and you will be like God…"* (Genesis 2: 16-17; 3:2-3).

When Adam and Eve ignored God's parental guidance and adopted the tempter's attitude that they could be "as God," they began to live and act independently of God and failed to respond as dependent children.

Since we are all endowed with free will, we can make our own choices. So we experience God's will for our life to the degree that we choose to partake of His fellowship and make our choices based on His will.

A question that evangelists like to ask people is, "Where will you spend eternity?" (What is often missing in evangelistic messages is that we can experience heaven and hell right here in this life.) The futuristic heaven/hell option is an appeal that generally encourages a response based on fear.

Bullies use fear to intimidate and control weaker individuals. Bullying is a huge problem today in our schools, neighborhoods, some churches, and even in families and places of work. This is contrary to our Father's love. God is not a bully, wanting to intimidate or control us.

God loves us, wants the best for us, and wants us to freely come to Him of our own choice. When love is used as the motivator for people to come to God, won't the resulting relationship with God be healthier? What if we emphasize how wonderful life can be here on earth when we are in full fellowship with God, our Father? It changes everything!

Perfect love casts out fear, so when we emphasize loving fellowship with God, fear will have no place in the conversation or in our response.

> *There is no fear in love; but perfect love casts out fear, because fear involves punishment, and the one who fears is not perfected in love* (1 John 4:18).

> *If anyone loves Me…We* [Father and Son] *will come to him, and make Our abode* [dwelling fellowship] *with him* (John 14:23).

As we converse with our Father, we assimilate His perspective and increasingly transform into His reflective resemblance. In other words, as we become more and more like Him, we reap the benefits of a life in today's world that is full of His love.

> *He who hears My word, and believes Him who sent Me, has eternal* [spirit] *life…has passed out of death into life* (John 5:24).

Submission to the Supreme

Yes, God's will is supreme, yet He gives us the freedom to choose when we respond and to what degree we partake of His will. God gives each of His offspring the ability and freedom to make a variety of choices: We can choose whom to marry, where to live, what to do for a living, and how we conduct our lives. He allows us to be selfish or selfless, uncaring or compassionate, rude or courteous. He even gives us the option to receive or reject His guiding presence.

Since free will is a feature God has given to all mankind, the will of God becomes more of our reality as we choose to submit to His will and ways. The will of God does not intend to restrict or limit our choices, but to provide better ones. God is more concerned about why we choose, than He is with what we choose to do. It is like the question asked of Jesus, "Who is my neighbor?" The answer was "go and be one" rather than qualifying who may be my neighbor. If we

Will of God Directs Us

are receiving His insightful guidance and becoming the godly person He desires us to be, the everyday choices we make will tend to be blessed by God.

Our free will is a blessing when we choose to follow the guidance of God's love in each of the choices we make. When we ignore the insightful guidance of the Giver of Life, our choices will tend to lead to deathly results. God provides a better way for us to relate.

> *Be transformed by the renewing of your mind, that you may prove* [make so] *what the will of God is* (Romans 12:2).

> *Put on the new self, who is being renewed to a true knowledge according to the image of the One who created...*(Colossians 3:10).

> *We...beholding...the glory of the Lord, are being transformed into the same image from glory to glory* (2 Corinthians 3:18).

God longs to share His perspective with us, so our heart's character, attitude, and personality can adjust into better reflective resemblances of His heart. Our fellowship with God allows us to partake of His insight regarding each of our life situations and circumstances.

The will of God for our life is simple: We are to be children who yield to the Father's insightful fellowship and learn to be better reflective resemblances of His heart. We want to stay attentive to His insightful guidance, every day.

This being said, we want to be open and receptive to what God may say today, in our present situations and circumstances. Again, Abraham is a good example: God instructed him to sacrifice his son Isaac and then later changed what He previously instructed. As developing children, we want to be flexible enough to sense God's guidance afresh for today.

Don't forget that Paul's fresh revelation of the Gospel added to and enlarged the perceptions of the other disciples, to include everyone without requiring that they become Jewish and practice the previous religion's customs (Acts 15:1-19). Our soft adjustment to God's "revealing will and ways" helps us become more mature children.

> *...that, in reference to your former manner of life, you lay aside the old self, which is being corrupted in accordance with the lusts of deceit, and that you be renewed in the spirit of your mind, and put on the new self, which in the likeness of God has been created in righteousness and holiness of the truth* (Ephesians 4:22-24).

As we choose to yield to the freshly revealed will of God, we find a peaceful rest for our troubled soul (Matthew 11:28-30). Our lives become full and rewarding when we mature into disciplined children of God who ask, seek, and knock regarding His will (Matthew 7:7). Isn't this something we all desire?

Memorize:

> *And do not be conformed to this world, but be transformed by the renewing of your mind, so that you may prove what the will of God is, that which is good and acceptable and perfect* (Romans 12:2).

Questions to consider:

1. What did God first declare to be His will for humanity?
2. What is the difference between offspring and children?
3. How do we experience the will of God?

Chapter 8

Purpose of Life Destines Us

"Being a veterinarian, I had been called to examine a ten-year-old Irish wolfhound named Belker. The dog's owners, Ron, his wife, Lisa, and their little boy, Shane, were all very attached to Belker, and they were hoping for a miracle.

"I examined Belker and found he was dying of cancer. I told the family we couldn't do anything for Belker and offered to perform the euthanasia procedure for the old dog in their home.

"As we made arrangements, Ron and Lisa told me they thought it would be good for four-year-old Shane to observe the procedure. They felt as though Shane might learn something from the experience. The next day, I felt the familiar catch in my throat as Belker's family surrounded him.

"Shane seemed so calm, petting the old dog for the last time that I wondered if he understood what was going on.

Purpose of Life Destines Us

Within a few minutes, Belker slipped peacefully away. The little boy seemed to accept Belker's transition without any difficulty or confusion.

"We sat together for a while after Belker's death, wondering aloud about the sad fact that animal lives are shorter than human lives. Shane, who had been listening quietly, piped up, 'I know why.'

"Startled, we all turned to him. What came out of his mouth next stunned me. I'd never heard a more comforting explanation.

"He said, 'People are born so that they can learn how to live a good life—like loving everybody all the time and being nice, right?' The four-year-old continued, 'Well, dogs already know how to do that, so they don't have to stay as long.'"
—*Author unknown*

> Preparation for old age should begin no later than one's teens. A life, which is empty of purpose until 65, will not suddenly become filled on retirement.
> —*Dwight L. Moody*

From time immemorial, people have asked: Why was I born? Is there a purpose for my existence? We ask these questions because deep within we desire to understand if there is a purpose we can pursue, instead of just existing and hoping for the best. Our real question is: Can I know and pursue my own unique purpose and destiny? This chapter will discuss the two deepest questions that humans have ever asked: Why are we here? And, why am I here?

Our first question can be answered by restating what has become clear in previous chapters: We are created to know and love God as Father, so we can become reflective resemblances of His heart CAP and love one another as His offspring and maturing children.

The second question about us is more complicated. However, if we do not see and build on the foundation of "why we are here," our personal purpose will miss a lot of defining value. God comes to us as a Spirit presence to share details on a more personal level.

> *But when He, the Spirit of truth comes, He will guide you into all the truth; for He will not speak on His own initiative, but whatever He hears, He will speak; and He will disclose to you what is to come* [your developing future] (John 16:13).

Heaven on Earth

You may ask, aren't we just killing time here on earth as we wait for the Celestial Express to whisk us out of this temporal realm? Isn't heaven where the real action happens? Actually, there is a spiritual purpose for our life on earth. We are intended to incorporate spiritual values into our natural life.

Our life involves the relational interaction of our natural body, our eternal spirit, our conscious soul, and our expressive heart. We all fundamentally have a body, a spirit, and a conscious awareness that enables us to receive input from and interact with both the natural and the spiritual realities.

Our life begins with a dominant awareness of natural needs. As we become aware of and respond to the stimulation of our spirit, life becomes more meaningful and significant. The spiritual side of our life incorporates eternal values and the in-depth reason for our existence.

Jon Meacham, writing in *Time Magazine* (April, 2012) offers insightful clarity to this issue in the following few paragraphs:

"If heaven is understood more as God's space on earth than as an ethereal region apart from the essential reality we know, then what happens on earth matters even more than we think, for the Christian life becomes a continuation of the unfolding work of Jesus.

"If you begin to think about the drama of life in such terms, you begin to invest more meaning in the here and now…The love of friends, the brush of your spouse's hand, and the eyes of a young child—these become not hints or glimpses of what heaven may be like as a posthumous region but of what earth is like as light and love achieve dominion over darkness and envy.

"This is a debate…about whether believing Christians see earthly life as inextricably bound up with eternal life or as simply a prelude to a heavenly existence elsewhere.

"If, like me, you find the former option intriguing, then heaven is the reality one creates in the service of the poor, the sick, the enslaved, the oppressed. It is not Disneyland in the sky but acts of selflessness and love that bring God's sacred space and grace to a broken world suffused with tragedy. We could do worse than think in such terms."

Spiritual and Natural People

The truth of the matter is, no one functions entirely as just a natural or spiritual person. We are all influenced by both realities. Everyone is swayed by natural events and desires. We are also influenced by spiritual events and inclinations.

We all choose which stimuli we respond to and the level of our response in each situation we encounter. When we are led by God's Spirit, we develop godly perceptions of what is true and real. Again, we choose our responses and can grow in our faith in God.

No one is beyond stepping outside of His guidance, entertaining misguided perceptions, and then acting wrongly. An example is found in King David. He was a physical and spiritual person, just like us. David sought the heart of God from childhood:

> *He* [God] *raised up David to be their king, concerning whom He also testified and said, "I have found David the son of Jesse, a man after My heart, who will do all My will* (Acts 13:22).

David's life story (1 Samuel 16 through 2 Samuel 24) illustrates how we can seek God in truth and righteousness and still be led astray by physical desires, even to the point of great sin:

> *Now when evening came David arose from his bed and walked around on the roof of the king's house, and from the roof he saw a woman bathing; and the woman was very beautiful in appearance. So David sent messengers and took her, and when she came to him, he lay with her* (2 Samuel 11:2-4).

Purpose of Life Destines Us

David fell under judgment for his actions, repented of his error, and continued to honor God. After David died, his son Solomon became king. In Solomon's prayer, he acknowledged God's love and favor on his imperfect father:

> *Then Solomon said, "You have shown great lovingkindness to Your servant David my father, according as he walked before You in truth and righteousness and uprightness of heart toward You"* (1 Kings 3:6).

In contrast, the attitude of the religious Pharisees in Jesus' day was so contrary to God's purpose that they were called children of opposition:

> *By this the children of God and the children of the devil are obvious: anyone who does not practice righteousness is not of God, nor the one who does not love his brother* (1 John 3:10).

> *You are of your father the devil, and you want to do the desires of your father…Whenever he speaks a lie, he speaks from his own nature, for he is a liar and the father of lies* (John 8:44).

Most of life's choices are not quite as dramatic or life changing as King David's. Most of us struggle with things such as whether or not to be kind to the rude checkout girl at the market, or deciding to return the extra cash when there is a checkout error. However, the way we treat unruly children, offbeat siblings, people we disagree with, and the least desirable among us, all demonstrate the level of our spirituality.

When Scripture refers to a natural or a spiritual person, it speaks of the most dominant perspective that influences our life. A spiritual person is most often guided by godly perspectives, although not always. While we are both natural and spiritual beings, our leaning in any moment can be toward natural or spiritual stimuli, in different times and situations:

> *The wisdom from above* [of God] *is first pure, then peaceable, gentle, reasonable, full of mercy and good fruits, unwavering, without hypocrisy* (James 3:14-17).

> *A natural man does not accept the things of the Spirit of God…they are spiritually appraised* (1 Corinthians 2:14).

Life is meant to include a care and concern for the well-being of our body, soul, and spirit. Our life experience is limited when we ignore or negate the importance of either reality.

The proper care and feeding of the natural and spiritual sides of our life are necessary for us to mature into the fullness of our heavenly Father's created purpose. We don't want to be so earthly minded that we miss God's intention, nor so heavenly minded that we're of no earthly good.

When we neglect our physical health, we do so to our own detriment. Science tells us that nearly every cell in our physical body changes at different rates every year. The body produces new cells from the nutrition we consume and provides one of three results: 1) it maintains our current health, 2) improves our health, or 3) deteriorates our health.

Allow me to digress a little: A day came when I realized that refined carbohydrates, which are processed in the body as sugars, complicate optimum health. To help me quit eating these tasty delights, I accepted the fact that they cause inflammation in our body and much like a poison, they invite disease. I didn't want to continue to poison myself so I began to reduce and eliminate them from my diet. It took a few months, but eventually I lost my craving for them. (I still enjoy a sweet treat occasionally and during holiday seasons.)

In the same way we should evaluate what we are feeding our spirits. Does what we read, watch on TV, or view on our computers poison our soul and downgrade the dominance of God's Spirit in our life? Let's pay attention and live with purpose so we can excel in each of our relationships.

Connecting Love

Getting back to our relationship with God, we want to see that love is more than what God does, love is who He is. His love directs every expression of His heart.

We can primarily see God as a loving Father that entices us to receive His care or we can visualize Him as a Judge who forces our obedience through instilling in us a fear of punishment. The perception of God that dominates our understanding affects how we act. What we believe does matter.

Jesus proclaimed that everything God has said to mankind over the centuries is intended to teach us to love Him as Father and to lovingly treat one another (Matthew 22:37-40).

> *Love is patient, love is kind and is not jealous; love does not brag and is not arrogant, does not act unbecomingly; it does not seek its own, is not provoked, does not take into account a wrong suffered, does not rejoice in unrighteousness, but rejoices with the truth; bears all…believes all …hopes all…endures all* (1 Corinthians 13:4-7).

> *Beloved, let us love one another, for love is from God; and everyone who loves is born of God and knows God* (1 John 4:7).

John indicates in his writings that our love for one another is evidence, in some measure, that we know and experience God. When we approach God and respond to Him as loving children, we are able to see His heart more clearly. This allows us to go beyond the ancient Israelite experience of just knowing the acts of God. As we come to really know our heavenly Father's heart, we tend to mature into better reflective resemblances of His loving heart.

Each of God's children are only bits, pieces, and portions of His divine reality. It's in the fellowship of His presence that we learn what His heart is really like.

You may ask, what is meant by the "fellowship of His presence"? The term speaks of the times we interact with God, and of the times we share the thoughts and ways of God with each other. Jesus spoke about the presence of God this way; "When two or more interact around the things of God, He will be in our midst" (Matthew 18:20). The fellowship of God's presence involves our interaction with God and with one another. This combination, together, is real fellowship.

We're all relatives of one another, some close and some distant. When we really believe this truth, our interactions will display more of a sense of loving brotherhood, even to unbelievers.

> *So then, while we have opportunity, let us do good to all people, and especially to those who are of the household of the faith* (Galatians 6:10).

Purpose of Life Destines Us

Of course, sometimes God's love can appear to be tough: It was God's love that sent Adam from the Garden of Eden so he and Eve would not eat of the Tree of Life as unrepentant people. The Father's action was not so much a punishing judgment but a show of His loving grace and mercy. Today, as it was with Adam, it is our lack of repentance that keeps us away from the loving care of our Father and the Tree of Life.

It is the love of God that connects everything together. When we live our lives as extensions of God's love, it becomes easier for everybody to begin to find their place in the family of God. Our love for one another is like glue—it connects our weaknesses and shortcomings to a greater good.

Have you ever worked on a difficult jigsaw puzzle—the kind where a lot of the colors are very similar? It can be a daunting project. Just when you think you've found the right color, the shape doesn't fit. Or, you're sure the shape is right, but the color or pattern is not a match.

Now imagine trying to assemble such a complicated jigsaw puzzle without the box cover—you know, the one that shows what the finished puzzle is supposed to look like? Now that's complicated!

Scripture can be like those puzzle pieces—you try everything you can think of to put the pieces together but to no avail. Then Jesus steps in as the "box lid" and not only tells you how it's supposed to look, he demonstrates it for all to see. God shows us the pattern we are designed to follow in the life of His unique Son, Jesus Christ.

Our faith agrees with God. *See Appendix VIII: "What Is Faith" on page 187.*

A Greater Perspective

One day, a professor entered the classroom and asked his students to prepare for a surprise test. They all waited anxiously at their desks for the exam to begin.

The professor handed out the exams with the test facing down, as usual. Once he handed them all out, he asked the students to turn over the papers.

To everyone's surprise, there were no questions—just a black dot in the center of the sheet of paper. The professor, seeing the expression on everyone's faces, told them the following: "I want you to write about what you see there." The students, confused, got started on the inexplicable task.

At the end of the class, the professor took all the exams, and started reading each one of them out loud, in front of all the students. All of them, with no exception, defined the black dot, trying to explain its position in the center of the sheet.

After all had been read and the classroom was silent, the professor explained. "I'm not going to grade you on this; I just wanted to give you something to think about. No one wrote about the white part of the paper. Everyone focused on the black dot—and the same happens in our lives.

"We all have a white piece of paper to observe and enjoy, but we always tend to focus on the dark spots. Our life is a gift given to us by God, with love and care. We always have reasons to celebrate—nature renewing itself every day, our friends around us, the job that provides our livelihood, and the miracles we see every day. So why do we insist on focusing only on the dark spot—the health issues that bother

Purpose of Life Destines Us

us, the lack of money, the complicated relationship with a family member, the disappointment in a friend?

"The dark spots are very small when compared to everything we have in our lives, but they're the ones that pollute our mind. Take your eyes away from the dark dots in your life. Enjoy the blessings of each moment that life gives you. We want to focus on the larger perspective."

God revealed two amazing insights when He appeared in the human life of Jesus Christ: 1) God is our heavenly Father. He lovingly forgives our waywardness and longs for us to allow Him to lead, guide, and teach us through this life experience. 2) God demonstrated His desire for us as children, in the Son-to-Father fellowship Jesus had with Him. Jesus listened to God and proceeded to say and do likewise.

As a Son in fellowship with Father, Jesus said:

> *The Son can do nothing of Himself, unless it is something He sees the Father doing; for whatever the Father does, these things the Son also does* (John 5:19).

There are two passages in Scripture, only two, which indicate God and His ways may be beyond our ability to understand. The Old Testament passage says the thoughts and ways of God are not like those of the rebellious house of Israel (Isaiah 55:8). The New Testament passage says the heart and ways of God are beyond our ability to fully fathom:

> *Oh, the depth of the riches both of the wisdom and knowledge of God! How unsearchable are His judgments and unfathomable His ways!* (Romans 11:33)

While the depths of God's wisdom and the knowledge of His

ways are beyond anyone's ability to fully understand, there are 43 passages in Scripture that clearly say we can know, keep, walk in, and teach the ways of God. Jesus said that all who seek can know the ways of God.

Ask, and it will be given…seek, and you will find (Matthew 7:7).

Behold…if anyone hears My voice and opens the door, I will come in to him and will dine with him, and he with Me (Revelation 3:20).

My sheep hear My voice, and I know them, and they follow Me; and I give eternal life to them (John 10:27-28).

Our personal fellowship with the Father enables us to express our concerns to Him and allows God to share His guiding insight with us. We can believe God exists and even serve God with our gifting, yet not be responsive to His guidance:

For though by this time you ought to be teachers, you have need again for someone to teach you…you need milk and not solid food. For everyone who partakes only of milk is not accustomed to the word of righteousness, for he is an infant. But solid food is for the mature, who because of practice have their senses trained to discern (Hebrews 5:12-14).

God invites us to not only believe but also to partake of His interactive fellowship, to draw from His insightful perspective, and learn His way of life. He instructed us to observe Jesus' life example as the truthful way to live. It is within our fellowship with Father and our fellowship with each other that we are transformed into God's intention.

Purpose of Life Destines Us

We are to grow up in all aspects into Him who is the head, even Christ...being fitted and held together by what every joint supplies each individual part, causes the growth of the body for the building up of itself in love (Ephesians 4:15-16).

We are called to be a part of something bigger than ourselves and live beyond our own self-interests as members of the body of Christ, as participating members of God's family.

In This Together

A kindly, old stranger was walking through the land when he came upon a village. As he entered, the villagers retreated to their homes, locking their doors and windows.

The stranger smiled and asked, "Why are you all so frightened? I am a simple traveler, looking for a soft place to stay for the night and a warm place for a meal."

"There's not a bite to eat in the whole province," he was told. "We are weak and our children are starving. Better keep moving on."

"Oh, I have everything I need," he said. "In fact, I was thinking of making some stone soup to share with all of you." He pulled an iron cauldron from his satchel, filled it with water, and began to build a fire under it. Then, with great ceremony, he drew an ordinary-looking stone from a silken bag and dropped it into the water.

By now, hearing the rumor of food, most of the villagers had come out of their homes or watched from their windows. As the stranger sniffed the "broth" and licked his lips in anticipation, hunger began to overcome their fear.

"Ah," the stranger said to himself rather loudly, "I do like a tasty stone soup. Of course, stone soup with cabbage—now that's hard to beat."

Soon a villager approached hesitantly, holding a small cabbage he'd retrieved from its hiding place, and added it to the pot.

"Wonderful!" cried the stranger. "You know, I once had stone soup with cabbage and a bit of salt beef as well, and it was a meal fit for a king."

The village butcher managed to find some salt beef…. And so it went, through potatoes, onions, carrots, mushrooms, and so on, until there was indeed a delicious meal for everyone in the village to share.

—From a Portuguese Fable, author unknown

What do you bring to the table? We not only have something to give, we have ourselves to contribute to one another's welfare!

Humanity started in the heart of God as a desire to have offspring that He could parent into reflective resemblances of His heart. He designed life on earth to be the process He would use to birth, grow, and bring His offspring into maturity. This is why we were born; it's our purpose, our destiny. The Father is deeply interested in our birth and our developing life experience—He has a stake in our destiny!

Destiny is defined as: a prescribed purpose, an intended result. Our created purpose, our destiny, and our intended result are all the same. Our destiny is intricately tied to our receptive fellowship with Father and with one another.

Purpose of Life Destines Us

How well do we relate? Will we be the type of people who pursue God with all our heart, soul, mind, and strength? Or will we just try to get by with the minimum involvement in our relational fellowship with Him and with each other?

While some of us tend to ignore and even distain our Father, some of us are in the habit of living on the outer edges of God's loving fellowship. We are in the family of God, but because we are distant from His intimate presence, we don't always reflect God's heart in our families, neighborhoods, or in the world.

Our human existence involves the interaction of each element of our being (body, soul, and spirit). In much the same way, our life needs the interaction of God and of one another. We are all a part of a much bigger picture. When we live life outside of fellowship, we tend to be overly influenced by self-centeredness and the insecurities that accompany it. We want to learn to see "me" in the context of "us." Our individual value is most always improved in the context of us.

A song written by Joy Becker articulates purpose quite well:

To be an expression of God, to be His voice in the earth;
To blend our voices together, and be joined in Him as one;
To express God's love unto men,
As sons to shine forth as new light;
To be this expression grant it we pray,
For we love Thee oh Lord and Thy ways.

Where is your journey taking you? We are all on a road to somewhere, even if it seems like we are stuck in neutral at times. Are we looking ahead to see what's around the next bend in the road, or are we always looking behind through the rearview mirror? Are we focusing on what God has done, or some day will do, or are we living in what God is doing today? (Revelation 1:8)

Life can be a very exciting experience when we understand "what" we are, "who" we are, and "why" we exist. We can all learn to pursue God's will and purpose for our life. We want to learn to live life with a relational focus so we appropriately fellowship with God and with one another.

Here are two ways we can express God's purpose for our life:

1. My purpose in this life is to learn to fully love our heavenly Father and become a loving expression of His heart CAP.

2. My destiny is to reflect as a mirror and resemble as a son the CAP of our heavenly Father wherever I am.

Memorize: *"The wisdom from above is first pure, then peaceable, gentle, reasonable, full of mercy and good fruits, unwavering, without hypocrisy"* (James 3:14-17).

Questions to Consider:

1. Why can we not fully know God as disconnected individuals?

2. Why do you think love is to be the primary motivator for our actions?

3. What are some of the benefits of our fellowship with God?

APPENDICES

I. Cold, Dark, and Evil

The following story is one that helps to illustrate how negative values are simply the absence of positive ones.

A university professor at a well-known institution of higher learning challenged his students with this question:

"Did God create everything that exists?" A student bravely replied, "Yes, he did!"

"God created everything?" the professor asked. "Yes, sir, he certainly did," the student replied.

The professor answered, "If God created everything, then God created evil. Since evil exists, and according to the principle that our works define who we are, then we can assume God is evil."

The student became quiet and did not respond to the professor's hypothetical definition. The professor, quite pleased with himself, boasted to the students that he had proven once more that the Christian faith is a myth.

Another student raised his hand and said, "May I ask you a question, professor?"

"Of course," replied the professor.

The student stood up and asked, "Professor does cold exist?"

"What kind of question is that? Of course it exists. Have you never been cold?"

The young man replied, "In fact, sir, cold does not exist. According to the laws of physics, what we consider cold is in reality the absence of heat. Every object is measurable when it has or transmits energy, and heat is what makes matter have or transmit energy. Absolute zero (-273 C, -460 F) is the total absence of heat, and all matter becomes inert and incapable of reaction at that temperature. Cold does not exist. We have created this word to describe how we feel if we have no heat."

The student continued, "Professor, does darkness exist?" The professor responded, "Of course, it does."

The student replied, "Once again you are wrong, sir; darkness does not exist either. Darkness is, in reality, the absence of light. Light we can study but not darkness. In fact, we can use Newton's prism to break white light into many colors and study the various wavelengths of each color. You cannot measure darkness. A simple ray of light can break into a world of darkness and illuminate it. How can you know how dark a certain space is? You measure the amount of light present. Isn't this correct? Darkness is a term used by man to describe what happens when there is no light present."

Finally the young man asked the professor, "Sir, does evil exist?"

Now uncertain, the professor responded, "Of course, as I have already said. We see it every day. It is in the daily examples of man's inhumanity to man. It is in the multitude of crime and

Cold, Dark, and Evil

violence everywhere in the world. These manifestations are nothing else but evil."

To this the student replied, "Evil does not exist, sir, or at least it does not exist unto itself. Evil is simply the absence of God. It is just like darkness and cold—words that man has created to describe the absence of light and heat. God did not create evil. Evil is the result of what happens when man does not have God's love present in his heart. It is like the cold that is felt when there is no heat or the darkness that looms when there is no light."

This is an urban legend that is sometimes attributed to Albert Einstein. Whatever the source, the information presented is correct.

We tend to think of cold, dark, and evil as anti-forces, as forces that fight heat, light, and good. In reality, they are not. When God created light, darkness was an indirect result, as evidence of the absence of visible light.

"The One forming light and creating darkness, causing well-being and creating calamity; I am the Lord who does all these." Isaiah 45:7

Cold, dark, and evil are features that occupy the void when there is a lack of heat, light, and good. The negative characteristics have no power of their own. A change always results when heat enters a cold region, when light invades darkness, and when God approaches evil. Our closeness to heat, light, and good is what keeps us from various degrees of cold, dark, and evil.

II. Body and Flesh

There are two completely different Greek words in our New Testament that are translated body and flesh. Scripture uses each of them in both a literal and a figurative sense.

The Greek word translated "body" is *soma*, which means: an organized whole, made up of many parts and members. Soma is simply a functioning material body.

The human body is a combination of several interior and exterior parts. It is a group of structured bones, internal organs, skin, and several functional systems.

God designed the human body to function as an important part of our life in this material earth. It houses our God-given spirit and provides input for our soul consciousness. Our body links us to the natural realm and enables our interaction with physical realities.

In contrast to our body, the Greek word translated "flesh" is *sarx*, which means: the external part of a body (as the skin), the outer covering of the body's collective group.

Skin and flesh do not include the inner organs, bones, and blood of the body. During the Old Testament days, the Israelites were instructed to eat only the outer meats of animals and exclude the inner blood and organs. Flesh is simply the outer visible covering of the body.

Our flesh is the most relatable part of our corporate body; it is what people see and touch.

Many Greek philosophers spoke of the human body as

though it were a bad thing. Neither the New Testament nor normal Greek usage does so.

Two thousand years ago the spoken word of God came into flesh (sarx), to live as Jesus Christ. The life He lived illustrated God's intention for us as people of flesh.

The Word became flesh, and dwelt among us, and we saw His glory…full of grace and truth (John 1: 14).

Jesus is recognized as living in the flesh without sin because he yielded his activity to his Father's guidance.

Jesus answered… "Truly, truly, I say to you, the Son can do nothing of Himself, unless it is something He sees the Father doing; for whatever the Father does, these things the Son also does in like manner" (John 5:19).

Our natural body with its flesh will eventually die and return to dust. Since we are much more than flesh and bones, our spirit and conscious soul continues into the eternal realm.

In the New Testament, a "body" can refer to a person with spirit, soul, and physical members. However, it may also speak of a collective group of believers that are responding to God's guiding presence.

So we, who are many, are one body in Christ, and individually members one of another (Romans 12:5).

Flesh is used in Scripture in a figurative manner to speak of our physical expressions and actions, be they godly or not. Jesus instructed us to eat his flesh (sarx) as though words and word expressive activity were the real bread of life:

Truly, truly, I say to you, he who believes has eternal life. I am the bread of life...I am the living bread that came down out of heaven; if anyone eats of this bread, he will live forever; and the bread also which I will give for the life of the world is My flesh (John 6:47-51).

Obviously, Jesus was not indicating we are to eat His literal flesh. This is a figurative use of the word. The words and activity of Jesus help us relate to God's heart. They are as nourishment to our efforts to live a godly life. We want to observe His example and be led by our Father.

This is eternal life, that they may know You, the only true God, and Jesus Christ whom You have sent (John 17:3).

As we partake of the life Jesus demonstrated and absorb His words, we partake of eternal life. To put it another way, when we reflect and resemble, through our thoughts and actions, the life that Jesus lived in the flesh, we experience an eternal quality of life here on earth.

Figuratively, flesh speaks of our physical expressions and actions. When we submit to God's Lordship, we become members of the body of Christ. When our activity is in concert with Christ (God's anointing presence), we are the visible flesh of Christ in the earth. People begin to see Christ in us.

Carnal Mind

God designed and created us to function with a physical body and its relatable flesh. So, he intends for us to think, interact, and live a natural life. There is however, a conflict going on in our mind for domination and control.

In scripture, "carnal and carnality" are the same as "flesh and fleshly"—they represent our physical interactions with people. Different translations tend to use these words interchangeably. The carnal and fleshly mind refers to thoughts that are not in concert with God.

The book of Romans tells us that when our mind is set on the flesh, it is carnal and competes with spiritual input. The mind set on the flesh tends to ignore God's direction.

> *...sending His own Son in the likeness of sinful flesh...He condemned sin in the flesh, so that the requirement of the Law might be fulfilled in us, who do not walk according to the flesh but according to the Spirit* (Romans 8:3-4).

> *For those who are according to the flesh set their minds on the things of the flesh, but those who are according to the Spirit, the things of the Spirit. For the mind set on the flesh is death, but the mind set on the Spirit is life and peace, because the mind set on the flesh is hostile toward God* (Romans 8:9-14).

When the carnal mind dominates our thinking, our flesh is able to run rampant and tends to control our actions. This type of activity is called fleshly. It ignores God's guidance.

King David was known as a man of God. His expressions and actions, for the most part, were godly. But when he saw Bathsheba, fleshly inclinations overcame what God taught him. Even the most godly among us are susceptible to the carnal mind and its fleshly thoughts:

> *Beloved, I urge you...to abstain from fleshly lusts which wage war against the soul* (1 Peter 2:11).

The warfare in our soul involves our mind's thoughts, our will's understandings, and our emotional feelings. The self-centered carnal mind tends to want to function without God's relational guidance. It can cause us to act like "mere men" who are void of spiritual guidance.

> *And I, brethren, could not speak to you as to spiritual men, but as to men of flesh, as to infants in Christ* [immature]. *I gave you milk to drink, not solid food; for you were not yet able to receive it. Indeed, even now you are not yet able, for you are still fleshly. For since there is jealousy and strife among you, are you not fleshly, and are you not walking like mere men?* (1 Corinthians 3:1-3)

While our flesh (sarx) is prone to passion and affections, we do not have to yield to sinful activity. As a man, Jesus dealt with these same thoughts and feelings but did not succumb to ungodly lusts.

When we negate God's guidance and his way of life, we tend to respond to our fleshly, carnal mind with its ungodly lustful inclinations, desires, and appetites. This can include many excesses such as greed, illicit sexual activity, and even overeating to appease one's appetites.

Flesh speaks of the natural side of our life, our physical interactions with our environment and with others. Paul said our brotherhood in Christ, under God's influence, causes us to cease to see each other only by the flesh (2 Corinthians 5:16). We learn to recognize one another through the eyes of the spirit.

When we follow God's lead, be it from the written Scriptures or the still small voice of His Spirit, our soul is not dominated by the carnal mind, nor do we function only as fleshly beings, as mere men.

III. Get Understanding

As a teenager, one time I was in a meeting and enjoying the message until the minister repeated the phrase, "You don't have to understand, just believe." I began to question why God would give us a mind that can reason and understand if He intended us to "just believe." It did not make sense to me. When the phrase was repeated a third time, I became a bit irritated and decided then and there that I would not be satisfied with such an approach to God and His ways.

I committed myself to seek to "understand" all that God would reveal. I was already studying the Bible and becoming familiar with Scripture. A few years later as I picked up the Bible to read, I began the practice of asking, "Lord, show me what I have not yet seen." My life continues to be an amazing journey of discovery.

> *God has looked down from heaven upon the sons of men, to see if there is any one who understands…*(Psalms 53:2).

When someone says "I don't see," it is usually a request for more information. When we say "I don't care," we admit we really do not want to know. The old saying "ignorance is bliss" is often quoted as a beloved excuse for not wanting to know or understand.

Our ability to understand is limited when we fail to consider new thoughts and ideas that may stretch our current perceptions. If we do not consider the value of a new thought, it can fade away without ever influencing us. When we seek to consider and understand new insights, we can gradually begin to understand how they apply and fit into our lives.

> *Give me understanding, that I may observe thy law… Your testimonies are righteous forever; give me understanding that I may live* (Psalms 119:34, 144).

When we understand why something exists and how it is designed to function, we are able to utilize it more fully. How well do we understand what we are and how we are designed to function as a human being?

If our experience teaches us that an ill behavior is normal, we tend to believe it's the right way to act even though it's not. A lack of understanding can complicate our ability to do what is best. Jesus referenced a lack of understanding when he said, "Father forgive them; for they do not know what they are doing" (Luke 23:34).

We gather information from the exercise of our natural and spiritual senses. Research sheds insight on just how they register the information we encounter and breaks it into percentages: we receive 83% of the information we process by sight; 11% by sound; 3.5% by smell; 1.5% by touch; and 1% by taste.

Considering these percentages, is it any wonder that we tend to say "seeing is believing"? Our ability to see natural and spiritual realities has a major impact on our ability to register information and develop understanding.

Research also reveals our ability to retain information is affected by how we receive it. We retain 10% of what we read, 20% of what we hear, 30% of what we see, 50% of what we see and hear, 70% of what we discuss, and 90% of what we repeat and do. We retain much more when we give expression to and apply a new insight to our lives.

Get Understanding

While each of us has the ability to absorb and retain information, and to develop understanding, some of us tend to retain better when we hear while others retain better by seeing. We all retain more when we see, hear, and give expression to (or act upon) new information.

Jesus instructed us not only to be open to inspirational thought but also to diligently ask, seek, and knock:

> *I say to you, ask, and it will be given to you; seek, and you will find; knock, and it will be opened to you. For…who asks, receives; and he who seeks, finds; and to him who knocks, it will be opened* (Luke 11:9-10)

While no one has the capacity to comprehend everything in the natural and spiritual realms, Jesus said we can understand in greater depths if we seriously seek. We should not accept and "just believe" everything we have been taught. The sincerity of our search has a great effect on what we come to understand to be true and real.

> *I have many more things to say to you, but you cannot bear them now. But when He, the Spirit of truth, comes, He will guide you into all the truth* (John 16:12-13).

God offers to enlighten each of us, so we can understand. Jesus admonished us to allow the Spirit of truth to lead and guide us into more than we currently know. God wants to show each of us greater truth and bring fuller understandings.

Our perceptions produce a lasting effect on our mental, emotional, and physical health. Our understanding of what is true and right exercises sway over what we eat, where we go, what we do in various situations, and how we treat each other.

George Washington Carver was a black man born into slavery. He went on to become one of the most prominent scientists and inventors of his time (early 1900s). He devised over 100 products from the peanut and formulated other very important products for the 20th century, like plastics and gasoline.

Late in life, George reported: "When I was young, I said, 'God, tell me the mystery of the universe.' But God answered, 'That knowledge is reserved for me alone.' So I said, 'God, tell me the mystery of the peanut.' Then God answered, 'Well, George, that's more nearly your size.'"

George was initially asking for insight that was beyond his ability to understand. When he humbly scaled his request back to what he could understand and what would be useful, God accommodated him.

We are all limited in some ways by our family circumstances and where we are raised, but we do not have to surrender to the self-imposed restrictions. More significantly, we limit ourselves by our lack of desire to seek and consider beyond what we already know.

We want to be receptive to all that God desires to share with us. When we diligently search, we begin to understand in greater degrees. Let us seek to discover so wisdom will come.

> *Oh, the depth of the riches both of the wisdom and knowledge of God!* (Romans 11:33)
>
> *For the LORD gives wisdom; from His mouth come knowledge and understanding* (Proverbs 2:6).

Wisdom is the application of understanding. When we desire

to understand and diligently seek insight, degrees of understanding will come and wisdom regarding its application results. Without God in our life, our wisdom is greatly limited.

Trust in the Lord with all your heart, and do not lean on your own understanding. In all your ways acknowledge Him (Proverbs 3:5).

What does Scripture mean by our own understanding? "Our own" refers to the thoughts and actions that ignore or seek to negate God and His input. Communism and socialism are examples. Both are rooted in the biblical concept of sharing but disdain God and negate His involvement. Consequently, they govern in ways that degrade life. When we consider God's input, everything makes more sense.

Most of our experiences stir thoughts and feelings. These conscious considerations are opportunities to process and absorb new insight into our developing consciousness. Scripture encourages us to observe, consider, and seek to understand.

With all your acquiring, get understanding (Proverbs 4:7).

Are we satisfied with passive or occasional involvement with God, our real source of understanding? Do we earnestly desire to understand what life is all about? Are we energetically pursuing more insight? Have you considered how fully water covers the sea?

But seek first His kingdom and His righteousness, and all these things will be added to you (Matthew 6:33).

For the earth will be filled with the knowledge of the glory of the LORD, as the waters cover the sea (Habakkuk 2:14).

IV. Attitude Rules

When we illustrate the heart as one of our triangles, attitude appears at the top feature of our expressive heart. Our attitude is the most important heart feature.

Scripture uses the word "heart" to speak of our character, attitude, and personality (CAP)—"who" we are as expressive beings. Attitude maintains the top place in our illustration because it colors and influences everything we say and do.

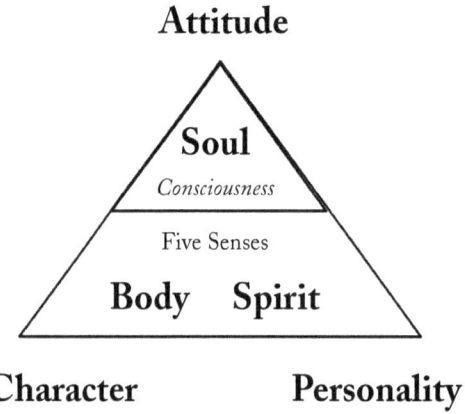

God amplified the importance of our heart's attitude when He sent the prophet Samuel to anoint David as king.

> *God sees not as man sees, for man looks at the outward appearance, but the LORD looks at the heart"* (1 Samuel 16:7).

Our heart's character and personality are both subject to the attitudes we entertain. Our attitudes exercise an amazing influence over who we really are as a person and maintain a certain rule over all our activities. Our attitudes permeate our entire being (body, soul, and spirit) to influence all our expressions.

Our responses in life are not so much about the circumstances but rather emanate from what we are made of. The same boiling water that softens the potato hardens the egg.

We may say the right words to someone in a difficult situation and our lack of sympathy (attitude) will cause what we say to come across as empty words. We can say "I really care" or "I love you" and our insincerity will make our words sound worthless.

One of the first stories in Scripture tells of Adam's sons Cain and Abel. When they brought offerings to God, he was not pleased with Cain. Because God's displeasure was not with what Cain offered, God instructed the Israelites later on to bring offerings from their crops. God looked beyond the offering and saw in Cain's heart an attitude that was amiss. God encouraged Cain to adjust his countenance (attitude) so sinful actions would not overtake him.

> *So Cain became very angry and his countenance fell. Then the LORD said to Cain, "Why are you angry? And why has your countenance fallen? If you do well, will not your countenance be lifted up? ...sin is crouching at the door... its desire is for you, but you must master it"* (Genesis 4:5-7).

Every time the NASB uses countenance, an attitude is attached: a sad..., a fallen..., troubled in..., haughtiness of..., an angry..., a fierce..., rebuke of..., and the light of God's countenance. Countenance refers to a visible expression of attitude. Cain responded to God's caution by killing Abel, and then fled from the influence of God's presence to dwell in the land of Nod.

It becomes obvious that Cain received his unrepentant attitude, at least in part, from his father. Adam lost his place in the Garden of Eden largely because he failed to repent of the attitude he adapted when he chose to ignore God's guidance.

Attitude infects what we think, feel, and believe (the activity of mind, will, and emotion) and then exercises influence over our expressive activity. Henry Ford referred to attitude this way; "Whether you think you can, or you think you can't—you're right." A can-do attitude or a defeatist attitude affects how well we do everything.

When we say, "My heart belongs to…(my spouse, my children, my friend, my country, my God)," we speak of allegiance, loyalty, and commitment. The attitude of our heart, both good and bad, tends to direct what we do and say, to support or to undercut our commitments.

This is why we want to be fully committed to God and his ways and not be half-hearted. Our attitude towards God affects how we perceive truth and what we believe to be reality. It can minimize our perception of God's care for us and make His love appear to be vague or negligible.

> *Therefore the LORD God of Israel declares…"For those who honor Me I will honor, and those who despise Me will be lightly esteemed"* (1 Samuel 2:30).

A negative attitude toward God, as Adam and Eve accepted, will seem to limit the demonstration of His love for us be-

Attitude Rules

cause we separate ourselves from His intimate care.

> *But your iniquities have made a separation between you and your God, and your sins have hidden His face from you so that He does not hear* (Isaiah 59:2).

While we can point to many apparent causes for our struggles, Scripture gives us a list of obvious core problems. The first in a list is generally the primary or most important one.

> *For our struggle is not against flesh and blood, but against the rulers, against the powers, against the world forces of this darkness, against the spiritual forces of wickedness in the heavenly places* (Ephesians 6:12).

The first, and thus primary, item listed is "rulers." The Greek word *arche* means: basic, underlying, foundational cause. The KJV translates the plural and singular of this Greek word eight times as "principality" and forty times as "beginning." Every time this word is used, it speaks of a beginning, a start, or an initial cause.

The primary causes we struggle with probably refer to the original thoughts that led our first parents away from God's guidance. The idea they accepted indicated we should be as God and rule ourselves. This planted an attitude that still tempts us to arrogantly act like we do not need God or anyone else.

It is helpful to realize that some attitudes are more surface level while some are very deep seated. Jesus gave us an example of two sons that demonstrates how surface attitudes can spark immediate responses while deep-seated attitudes eventually win out.

> *A man had two sons, and he came to the first and said, "Son, go work today in the vineyard." And he answered, "I will not"; but afterward he regretted it and went. The man came to the second and said the same thing; and he answered, "I will, sir"; but he did not* (Matthew 21:28-30).

Scripture instructs us to resist the devil and the temptations to ignore our heavenly Father (James 4:7). When we entertain such thoughts, they infect our consciousness, take root, and then can become as oppressive overlords. Our deepseated attitudes affect everything we say and do.

Godly attitudes are life-giving while others tend to be destructive. The real battle of the ages is the battle for our soul (our mind, will, and emotion). Our soul consciousness is the incubator (breeding place) and primary launching pad for expressive attitudes. This conflict rages in every person.

> *Do nothing from selfishness…with humility of mind regard one another as more important than yourselves; do not merely look out for your own personal interests, but also for the interests of others. Have this attitude in yourselves which was also in Christ Jesus* (Philippians 2:3-5).

The remarkable thing is that we have the choice to create our attitude. We cannot change our past, the way people act, or the inevitable. We can, however, change our attitude.

How can we change our attitude and become better reflections of our heavenly Father? It begins with a desire. Do we desire to be and do better? If so, we allow God to transform what we think, what we feel, and what we believe. God is more than willing. The question is, are we willing?

Attitude Rules

Does our heart attitude appear to others as hateful or loving, demanding or thankful, obstinate or adjustable, suspicious or trusting, arrogant or gracious, insecure or confident, victimized or overcoming, condemning or forgiving?

Scripture gives us a gold standard for God's attitudes.

But the fruit [expressions] *of the Spirit* [of God] *is love, joy, peace, patience, kindness, goodness, faithfulness, gentleness, self-control* (Galatians 5:22-23).

When these attitudes become ours, they make all the difference in the world and equip us to be more than overcomers.

V. Mature Not Perfect

There are several verses in Scripture that appear to encourage us to be perfect. The most obvious one is:

Therefore you are to be perfect, as your heavenly Father is perfect (Matthew 5:48).

When we consider that God alone has no beginning or ending and that He alone is able to be present everywhere, we see this verse is not saying that we are to be as God's essence. We are constantly growing, maturing, and changing (as we should) while God remains the same, so we cannot become wholly perfect like God. Consequently, the above verse must speak of something else.

The first recorded statement God made about mankind proclaimed that we are intended to be made into the image and likeness of God (Genesis 1:27). We must ask, what is this image and likeness we are designed to be? It obviously has nothing to do with a physical appearance, an ability to stand upright, or a communicative ability. All humans and many animals are endowed with such abilities.

The image and likeness of God really speaks of the heart character, attitude, and personality that we are intended to reflect and resemble.

In mankind's beginnings, God told Adam and Eve to not partake of one tree. When they were tempted by the idea that they could "be like God and know everything from good to evil," they ignored God's guidance and accepted a different perception of God's stated purpose.

Mature Not Perfect

Then, as God promised, their close fellowship with the Father ceased (Genesis 2:16-17). When they submitted to "knowing" through the variables of good and evil, their ability to clearly hear and respond to God's insightful lead was compromised. Apart from God's guidance, we live in sin's separation as dead people.

The image and likeness of God we are created to experience does not relate to our ability to reason, discern, and learn by experience. Even in fellowship with God, we do not always make the right choices. To amplify the death they chose, God removed them from the Garden of Eden so they would not eat of the Tree of Life in their unrepentant condition.

In what form or fashion are we to be as our heavenly Father? Clarity comes when we realize the word "perfect" is translated inappropriately from the Greek word *teleios*. In the *Hebrew-Greek Key Study Bible*, the scholar Spiros Zodhiates defines the Greek teleios as:

> Adult, full-grown, of full age as opposed to little children. God's perfection is absolute; man's is relative reaching the goal set for him by God with each individual different according to one's God-given ability...Teleios is not to be confused with anamartetos, without sin or sinless.

In other words, to be perfect (teleios) really speaks of us reaching a goal, completing a process, and finishing a cycle. It refers to the process of completing levels of maturity. There is an indication that the finishing of teleios is preparatory to entering other stages or processes, like seeds maturing into plants that continue to grow and children mature into adults who continue to age and mature. Life continues and we face a variety of trying situations, never as perfect beings, but as more mature children of God.

The KJV usually translates teleios as "perfect," but in one place it did not:

> *But strong meat belongeth to them that are of full age* [teleios], *even those who by reason of use have their senses trained to discern good and evil* (Hebrews 5:14).

The NASB version translates teleios as "mature" four times and "complete" two times. The context of these verses confirms the word is concerned with levels of maturity rather than errorless perfection.

> *Brethren, do not be children in your thinking; yet in evil be infants, but in your thinking be mature* (1 Corinthians 14:20).

> *But solid food is for the mature, who because of practice have their senses trained to discern…* (Hebrews 5:14).

> *Until we all attain to the unity of the faith, and of the knowledge of the Son of God, to a mature man, to the measure of the stature…of Christ* (Ephesians 4:13).

> *Yet we do speak wisdom among those who are mature; a wisdom, however, not of this age…* (1 Corinthians 2:6).

> *We proclaim Him, admonishing…teaching…so that we may present every man complete in Christ* (Colossians 1:28).

> *Jesus said to him, "If you wish to be complete, go and sell…and come, follow Me"* (Matthew 19:21).

The following instance is one of 13 times the NASB translates teleios as "perfect." Notice how the text verifies that the word actually speaks of a level of maturity:

> *But when the perfect comes, the partial will be done away. When I was a child, I used to speak like a child, think like a child, reason like a child; when I became a man, I did away with childish things* (1 Corinthians 13:10-11).

Why is this important? Perfect and mature refer to different ideas. Humans are unable, at least in this life, to be perfectly errorless. We can however, enter levels of maturity. Obviously we want to be on our best behavior, but even our best discerning behavior can miss the mark.

Take a moment and consider this instruction from Jesus. In context, it speaks of loving our enemies as God loves them.

> *But I say to you, love your enemies and pray for those who persecute you, so that you may be sons of your Father who is in heaven; for He causes His sun to rise on the evil and the good, and sends rain on the righteous and the unrighteous...Therefore you are to be perfect, as your heavenly Father is perfect* (Matthew 5:44-48).

We want to come to a level of maturity so we can love as our heavenly Father loves. Yes, some of our brothers are close and some are distant, while some are really out there. Nevertheless, we are all God's offspring even if we do not respond to His love as children of God. We are family.

> *We have fixed our hope on the living God, who is the Savior of all men, especially of believers* (1 Timothy 4:10).

We are all intended to partake of His guiding presence and mature as children of God.

VI. Called and Chosen

While we are invited to interact with God, we choose when we respond and to what degree we partake of our heavenly Father's insightful fellowship.

We can accept God's call to fellowship and experience a relational rebirth yet fail to realize our awakening is meant to activate fellowship with Him. We can be confident of a life after this life and yet be complacent about an active interaction with God in this world. We may even receive insights from God and respond as a faithful servant and still miss the insightful sharing that comes from a fellowship of hearts.

God loves each of His offspring so He blesses the just as well as the unjust (Matthew 5:45). Abundant blessings fall upon all who partake of God's fellowship and go from childhood disciplines to mature friendship.

> *You are My friends if you do what I command you. No longer do I call you slaves, for the slave does not know what his master is doing; but I have called you friends, for all things that I have heard from My Father I have made known to you* (John 15:14-15).

The story Jesus told of the Prodigal Son is a good example of the different levels of relationship we can have (Luke 15:11-32). Some of us take the gifts that God bestows, ignore Him, and live our own way. Others awaken from indifference and turn to partake of God's forgiving love. Some are raised in the house of God and fail to get close enough to our heavenly Father to understand His heart. Still others partake of God's richly rewarding insight and learn of his heart.

Too often we hear or read about the biblical heroes of faith and fail to really relate to them, as though that kind of faith was only for them and a few select people. We disassociate ourselves from them, thinking they were specially picked and chosen. We think they are not like us. This is a huge mistake.

Our general view of Jesus is an example of such disconnect. Scripture says he was tempted in all points like us (Hebrews 4:15), but we tend to say that the reason he didn't fall was because he was the Son of God. Disconnect! Being tempted, however, means Jesus could have been led astray.

Contrary to some views, when Jesus walked the earth, he did not know everything. He overcame temptations because he was in fellowship with Father and followed God's lead. Jesus did not stray from what God said (Matthew 4:1-11) and is God's example of what life in our heavenly Father's fellowship is really like. He followed Father's insightful lead.

It was his fellowship with his Father that enabled Jesus to say and do what he saw and heard the Father say and do (John 5:19). Close fellowship with his Father enabled Jesus to reflectively resemble God, even in the toughest of times, such as at his crucifixion (Matthew 26:39-42).

We are all called to know our heavenly Father and the fellowship of Christ (His anointing presence), as Jesus did.

> *If anyone serves Me, he must follow Me…if anyone serves Me, the Father will honor him* (John 12:26).
>
> *Therefore be imitators of God, as beloved children; and walk in love, just as Christ also loved you* (Ephesians 5:1-2).

As offspring, we are all invited and called to receive of God and experience the fellowship of His presence. While we are not all called into a major social activity, we are all called to reflectively resemble God (His image and likeness) in each of our situations and circumstances.

Scripture speaks of this calling as "adoption." In Hebrew society an adoption is called a bar mitzvah. Sons were raised primarily by their mother, and at the age of twelve they were adopted by their father. Dad then became the sons' primary teacher. Their father would educate the sons in a trade and discipline them in the ways and methods of the father so the sons could learn to function as a representative of the father.

> *God sent forth His Son, born of a woman…that we might receive the adoption as sons* (Galatians 4:4-5).

> *In love He predestined us to adoption as sons through Jesus Christ to Himself* (Ephesians 1:4-5).

> *All who are being led by the Spirit of God, these are sons of God. For…you have received a spirit of adoption as sons by which we cry out, "Abba! Father!"* (Romans 8:14-15)

In adoption we become more than offspring who know God as Provider, Lord, King, and Judge. We become children who are disciplined in the ways of the Father.

> *There was the true Light which, coming into the world, enlightens every man…As many as received Him, to them He gave the right to become children of God* (John1:9, 12).

Now the question is, how do we become chosen ones? John shares the secret of God's choosing: Those who are with Him are the called, chosen, and faithful (Revelation 17:14). The chosen are offspring who respond to God's call to become disciplined children and then remain faithful to the guiding fellowship of His presence.

Peter said that we make our calling and choosing certain, as we, by His grace and peace, become partakers of the divine nature (2 Peter 1:4, 10). Each of us diligently makes certain God's choosing by being faithful to His guidance.

Peter goes on to say that our conscious efforts to make certain our choosing means we are adding to our faith the qualities of moral excellence, knowledge, self-control, perseverance, godliness, brotherly kindness, and divine love (2 Peter 1:1-11).

Jesus became our elder brother (Romans 8:29), as one of us, so we would have a visual example to learn from. Jesus is a faithful reflective resemblance of our heavenly Father. We want to keep our eyes on the example God gave in Jesus and encourage each other to faithfully pursue God's guiding presence.

While Scripture tells us many are called but few are chosen (Matthew 22:13), we are also told the few will eventually become the many because the knowledge and glory of the Lord will fill the whole earth as the waters cover the sea (Habakkuk 2:14). While the waters do not fully cover the earth, their coverage of the seas is total and without exception.

In the fellowship of Father's presence, we are taught, apprenticed, tutored, and disciplined as maturing children into God's character, attitude, and personality (CAP).

Finally, all offspring are called to become disciplined children who reflectively resemble our heavenly Father in this life. Faithfulness to God's fellowship is what assures our choosing.

VII. Light of Life

Scripture defines God as the Eternal Spirit, the One who existed before time began and will exist after time passes. God is the Spirit Being that created this vast time, space, and matter universe that we are born into, live in, and in many ways are confined to.

God is the Eternal One who has no beginning or ending. He is ever-present, all-powerful, always mindful, and cannot be seen by natural eyes (omnipresent, omnipotent, omniscient, and invisible).

How can anyone relate to such an Entity? Scripture helps us relate to God by identifying an intricate part of His essence as Light.

God is Light, and in Him there is no darkness (1 John 1:5).

To understand God as Light, it is helpful to consider the natural sun. The sun creates and provides light that allows our natural eye to see and observe many of the features of the natural realm. Although we cannot see into the sun or fully comprehend its essence, we know it exists because we observe its expressive light.

Then God said, "Let there be light"; and there was light (Genesis 1:5).

The light in the creation account was not the natural sun and moon, which are not mentioned until the fourth creative cycle in verses 14-19. As a first creative action, God turned on the light of illumination, so that understanding could be achieved. God made a distinction between insightful light and its lack: dark obscurity.

Insightful light originates with God and flows from Him as revealing insight. Revealing light overcomes the darkness in any situation or circumstance. Jesus said the light of God's presence eventually reveals all that is secret, hidden, and unknown.

> *For there is nothing concealed that will not be revealed, or hidden that will not be known* (Matthew 10:26).

Since God is Light and He shares His revealing light, all enlightenment originates and comes from Him. Any other light source is really just a reflection of the light that is God—much like the light of the moon is merely a reflection of the light of the sun.

Like the natural sun, no one can fully comprehend the essence of God. We can, however, begin to understand and relate to Him through His expressions. Two thousand years ago God shared a unique expression of His Light in the life of Jesus Christ.

> *In Him was life, and the life was the Light of men* (John 1:4).

> *For God…is the One who has shone in our hearts to give the Light of the knowledge of the glory of God in the face of Christ* (2 Corinthians 4:6-7).

> *There was the true Light which, coming into the world, enlightens every man* (John 1:9).

Jesus demonstrated what the image and likeness of God is like.

I am the Light of the world. He who follows Me...will have [experience] *the Light of life* (John 8:12).

We are all birthed into this time and space realm so we can grow and develop as children of God. Our heavenly Father wants each one of us to receive and partake of His light so we learn to be images and likenesses (reflections and resemblances) of His heart's character, attitude, and personality (CAP).

God sent Jesus into the earth so we could better comprehend and relate to Him as the Light of our life. Jesus revealed the insight that God loves us and forgives us. He desires to be our guiding ligh and teach us how to live and mature as His children.

The Old Testament sheds some light on God's intention for our life. A short list of the graphic ways people in the Old Testament experienced God is found in chapter 11 of the book of Hebrews.

The New Testament illustrates the life and words of Jesus Christ and his disciples. We are all intended to receive the Light of Life and learn to live godly lives.

God...called us with a holy calling...according to His own purpose and grace which was granted us in Christ Jesus from all eternity...who...brought life and immortality to light through the gospel (2 Timothy 1:9-10).

But we all, with unveiled face, beholding as in a mirror the glory of the Lord, are being transformed into the same image from glory to glory... (2 Corinthians 3:18).

We know that the Son of God has come, and has given us

understanding so that we may know Him who is true; and we are in Him who is true, in His Son Jesus Christ. This is the true God and eternal life (1 John 5:20).

Since we all have spirit as part of our makeup, we are all equipped with spiritual senses that enable us to see, hear, touch, taste, and even smell the presence of God among us. The spiritual side of our five senses enables us to observe what God is saying and doing.

But solid food is for the mature, who because of practice have their senses trained to discern good and evil (Hebrews 5:14).

When we observe the life of Jesus and partake of the fellowship of the Father that he exampled, we really begin to understand and experience God as the Light of our life. Everyone has the capacity to receive and absorb of God's light-giving life. Greater depths of light come as we experience the fellowship of His presence. We are all designed to be reflective resemblances of God and conveyers of His light.

Those who have insight will shine brightly like the brightness of the expanse of heaven, and those who lead the many to righteousness, like the stars (Daniel 12:3).

The spirit of life in us equips each person to become reflective resemblances (image and likeness) of our heavenly Father. As we allow the Light of life to penetrate our soul consciousness (the activity of our mind, will and emotion), we are progressively transformed into the desire of God's heart, into disciplined children of God who reflect and resemble His heart CAP.

> *Now you are Light in the Lord; walk as children of Light…all things become visible when they are exposed by the light. For this reason it says, "Awake, sleeper, and arise from the dead, and Christ will shine on you"* (Ephesians 5:8, 13-14).

> *You are the light of the world…Let your light shine before men in such a way that they may see your good works, and glorify your Father* (Matthew 5:14, 16).

> *The path of the righteous is like the light of dawn that shines brighter and brighter* (Proverbs 4:18).

Everyone perceives in some degree that God really does exist, even those who openly deny Him. Just a slight awareness of His reality positions us to receive more insightful light. We want to seek to experience the presence of God and draw from the primary source of light, the Light of our life.

Jesus Christ is the first fully true-to-the-design son of God. He clearly demonstrated and taught that we, as offspring submitted to Father's tutoring, can hear and observe what God is saying and doing. Are we listening?

The Light of God becomes more visible in the culture of Christ, where God dwells among us, with us, and in our midst.

VIII. What Is Faith?

Many of us wonder about faith. We may even wonder why we don't seem to have enough faith to receive what we ask for. So, what is faith and how does it really function?

Faith is a word often used to identify a belief or a system of thought, which provides guidance. For instance, we might hear someone ask, "Of what faith are you?" Or, we may be encouraged to "Keep the faith." In each case, faith is used as a noun and identified as a belief system.

Scripture, however, uses "faith" as an action word. Scriptural faith is an activity that originates with God, who gives it to us as a gift.

God has allotted to each a measure of faith (Romans 12:3).

Scriptural faith is activated in us when a word or inspirational thought is received from God. We exercise faith when we accept what God says to us and allow it to become a confident persuasion. Faith helps us to know the word we hear is, or will eventually be, so.

For this article we will expound on the biblical definition of faith as a gift from God that is exercised as we agree with Him.

God has given spirit to every person. We generally call it the spirit of life. Scripture teaches us that this spirit is in every person, as a gift from God, one that enables our communication with Him, and that eventually returns to Him. This is true even when one does not acknowledge God or give oneself to interacting with Him.

As God has given spirit to everyone, He also gives us faith. The come-from and return-to God characteristic of our spirit is also a characteristic of faith. Faith is a value in each of us that is activated when we hear and accept an inspirational thought from God. Faith enables us to stand with what God says and desires us to do.

So, faith comes from hearing, and hearing by the word of Christ (Romans 10:17).

The word "Christ" is used correctly in this verse in *The Message, NASB, J.B Phillips,* and *The Emphasized Bible* translations. The Greek word that is translated "Christ" means "anointed." When a spoken or written word is quickened and comes alive to you, it may very well be a word of Christ, an anointed word from God that is intended for you.

Faith is the assurance of things hoped for, the conviction of things not seen (Hebrews 11:1).

Faith is a confident persuasion that supports a word that comes alive in your moment. Another way to translate the above verse is:

Faith is a confident expectation; the persuasion of what is not yet visible (Hebrews 11:1 – my version).

A word from God can refer to what is not yet visible in our time or space. If a word you hear or read is not quickened to/in you, it may not be the word of God for you or for your current situation. Not all words spoken by God are for everyone or for every moment.

When Peter saw Jesus walk on water he asked for a word. When Peter heard Jesus say "Come," his faith activated and

What Is Faith?

Peter walked on water. Others may have heard the word, but it was not spoken to them and there is no indication that Peter ever experienced this miracle again. The word given was only for Peter in that moment.

Faith keeps a delayed reality from seeming to be impossible. Abraham is called the father of the faithful (Romans 4:11-13). When God told Abraham he would have a son that would become a great nation, Abraham's faith was activated and provided levels of stability during the years there was no son.

After Isaac was born and had become a young man, God asked Abraham to offer up the promised son as a sacrifice. Upon Abraham's obedience, God's word to him changed. God instructed him to not do what He was previously told to do.

As with Abraham, our faith in God will help us hear a word that might be different from a previous instruction. Faith is based on what God is saying and desiring to accomplish now. Faith is activated to align us with His will for our time. Are we hearing Him for today?

Without faith it is impossible to please Him (Hebrews 11:6).

I am not ashamed of the gospel...For in it the righteousness of God is revealed from faith to faith; as it is written, "But the righteous man shall live by faith" (Romans 1:16-17).

Not everything in Scripture is appropriate for us, or for each of our moments. Living by faith requires an open and willing response to God and His guidance. We experience the righteousness of God from faith to faith, from one hearing and obedient action to another.

Scripture defines faith as our agreement with what God is saying and doing, to such a degree, that we seek to say and do likewise.

> *Faith, if it has no works, is dead...faith without works is useless...For just as the body without the spirit is dead, so also faith without works is dead* (James 2:17-26).

We can hear, believe, but then not function in agreement with the quickened word. If we believe what God says and our actions do not follow suit, our faith is inactive, as though it were dead.

Faith is activated and experienced when we hear a quickened word and act in agreement with it. The power of scriptural faith is in our agreement and active obedience to God's quickened word for our moments.

Israel's lack of faith kept that delivered generation from entering the promised life. They died in the wilderness. Faith helps us maintain a confidence in God's ability to accomplish what He says.

> *Jesus said to them, "Do you believe that I am able to do this?" They said to Him, "Yes, Lord."...Then He touched their eyes, saying, "It shall be done to you according to your faith"* (Matthew 9:28-29).

The apostles said to the Lord, "Increase our faith!" And Jesus said, "If you had faith like a mustard seed, you would say to this mulberry tree, 'Be uprooted and be planted in the sea'; and it would obey you" (Luke 17:5-6 see also verses 1-4).

In the above passage from Luke, Jesus taught the disciples to forgive no matter how often they were offended. This was hard to believe, so they asked Jesus for more faith. The response of Jesus clarified that it is not the *amount* of faith, but the *certainty* of faith. Faith is practiced as we confidently walk in what God is saying. So we simply forgive.

When a centurion asked Jesus to intervene for the health of his servant, he asked for a healing word because he knew that those under authority do what they are told. Jesus called this "great faith" (Luke 7:1-9). Faith involves our hearing and our agreeing action.

We want to realize that the exercise of our faith is not the same as believing. Beliefs are based on a trust in something or someone. Motivational speakers explain very effectively how our belief can influence outcomes. Our belief wires us to begin to receive and accomplish what we believe. There is no question about it, beliefs are very powerful—be they right, wrong, or somewhere in-between.

For instance, Adam and Eve accepted a deceptive thought in the Garden of Eden that changed their belief. The new belief system that guided their actions no longer agreed with God. Like our first parents, we can be led astray, believe in error, and lose our faith.

While faith includes believing, it is not founded on a belief that God will do what we ask. We can fully believe God will do what we want until we are blue in the face and still not receive it. If what we ask for is not aligned with what God is saying and desiring to do, we ask amiss. Faith's exercise will agree with God!

Now this is the confidence that we have in Him, that if

we ask anything according to His will, He hears us (1 John 5:14).

Some of the trials we go through are intended to try (to strengthen) our faith in God. The Epistles continually instruct us to encourage, strengthen and build-up one another's faith (Colossians 2:7; 1 Peter 5:10). In other words, we are to stir-up, establish, and add to faith. We want everyone to realize they can hear God and trust His word.

While God hears our prayers, we are cautioned about presuming that we can instruct God.

> *For through the grace given to me I say to everyone among you not to think more highly of himself than he ought to think; but to think so as to have sound judgment, as God has allotted to each a measure of faith* (Romans 12:3).

The above verse tells us the exercise of faith is connected to what we think, to sound judgment, and to our self-esteem. This passage provides an important insight. When we think we can instruct God or influence Him, we may be thinking too highly of ourselves.

> *Will the one who contends with the Almighty correct him? Let him who accuses God answer him!* (Job 40:2)

Our prayers are not efforts to influence God but to proclaim our desire to see God's best come into our situation. Prayers are to encourage, strengthen, and build-up faith and trust in God and His perspective regarding our needs and wants. Faith is always enriched with, "Not my will but God's be done" (Luke 22:42).

We want to ask God for what we want to have but always re-

What Is Faith?

member to trust He will do what is best for all involved. Faith is activated to help us stand in difficult times. Our faith exercise will glorify God and not ascribe any credit to us or our prayer as though we made it happen.

So, the exercise of faith will not always agree with what God speaks to someone else, nor with what God may have said to us in the past. God does not change but His word to us can. When we exercise faith, we are actively agreeing with what God is saying now and desiring to do in our time and moment.

Faith is a complex concept but it is so simple a child can understand it. Scriptural faith comes from God and enables us to hear, believe, and act in agreement with what God says and desires to do.

Faith comes from hearing…the word of Christ (Romans 10:17).

Faith is the assurance of things hoped for, the conviction of things not seen (Hebrews 11:1).

Scriptural faith arises as we are quickened by a word from God. Faith is a confident assurance that what God says is, or will be.

May our daily prayer be:

> *Heavenly Father, thank You for this day.*
> *May I be a better listener to Your voice, and*
> *A better observer of what You are doing, so*
> *I can be a better reflective resemblance of*
> *Your character, attitude, and personality.*

About the Author

Keith dedicated his life to our heavenly Father in his pre-teen years. During the teenage years, he became a strong student of the Scriptures. At 29 he married Nancy, and they have three children and five grandchildren.

Keith has ministered in a variety of Christian denominations, serving in many capacities including senior pastor.

For more than 20 years, Keith has helped authors with his warm, easygoing style in such publishing positions as Author/Editor Liaison, Director of Acquisitions, Assistant Publisher, and Literary Agent.

To contact Keith Carroll by email:
keith@RelationalGospel.com

or write to:
Keith Carroll
PO Box 428
Newburg, PA 17240

For Additional Resources...

Please visit:
http://relationalgospel.com
where you can find:

• An online presentation of *Created to Relate*, blog articles, and our other books. This site is perfect for sharing with others.

• A downloadable Leader's Resource Packet for a one-time $27 fee (free with a bulk order of 6 or more books). Our Leader's Packet includes expanded group discussion questions (12 to 14 per chapter), before and after participant evaluation forms, and tips on how to bring out the best in your group, all of which can be freely copied for group use and/or more intensive individual examination. Your purchase of the Leader's Packet (or 6 or more copies of the book) grants you unlimited photo copying rights of the included materials for your church or small group use.

• Information on purchasing printed and ebook copies of *Created to Relate*, including substantial discounts on bulk quantities.

www.ingramcontent.com/pod-product-compliance
Lightning Source LLC
Chambersburg PA
CBHW050635300426
44112CB00012B/1812